DAVID
FIVE HUNDRED YEARS

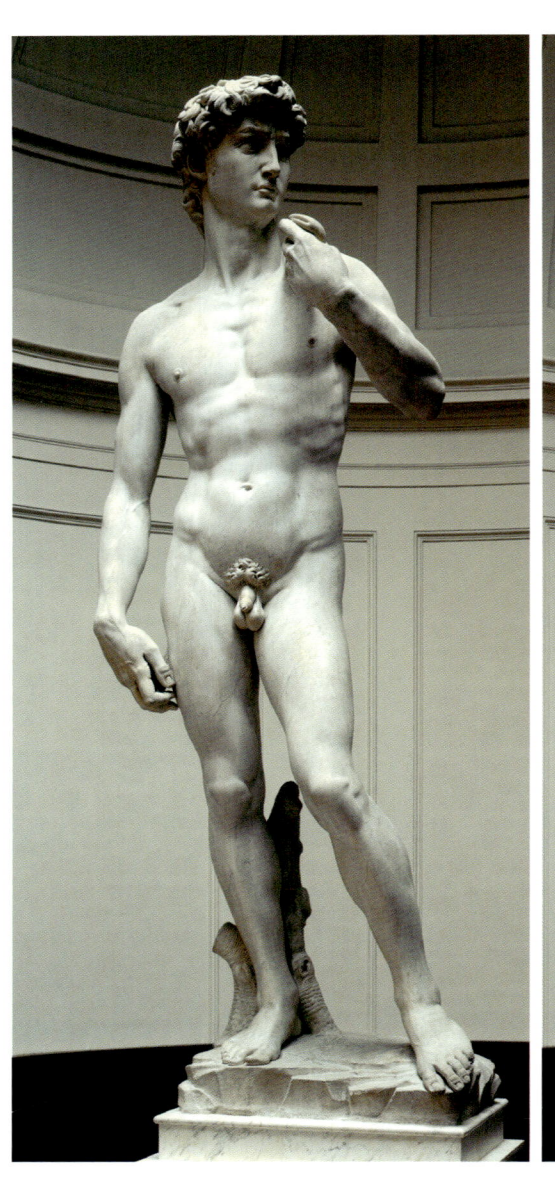
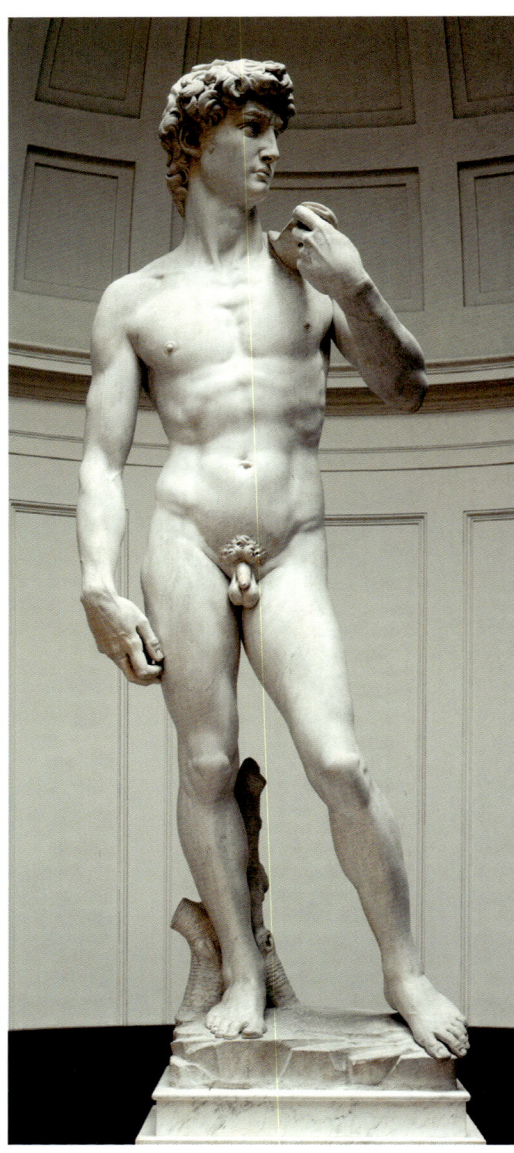
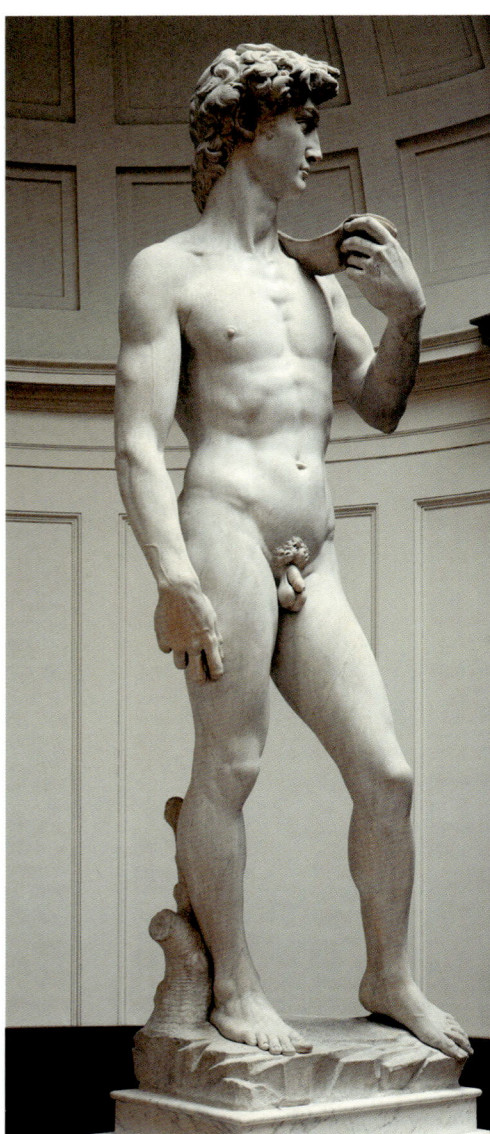

DAVID

FIVE HUNDRED YEARS

introduced and edited by
Antonio Paolucci

texts by
Cristina Bucci, Chiara Lachi

SCALA

© 2006 by SCALA Group S.p.A.

All rights reserved. No part of this publication may be reproduced, stored in a retrieval system, or transmitted, in any form or by any means, electronic, mechanical, photocopying, recording, or otherwise, without prior written permission from the publisher.

ISBN 978-88-8117-103-3

Translation: Huw Evans
Editing: Maria Caterina Pincherle

Photographic acknowledgments: SCALA Picture Library (S. Lampredi) except for page 15, SCALA/Bildarchiv Preussischer Kulturbesitz, Berlin; pages 78-79, Antonio Quattrone, Firenze

The images from the SCALA Picture Library that reproduce cultural assets owned by the Italian State are published by kind permission of the Ministry for Cultural Heritage and Activities

Printed by Lito Terrazzi, Florence, 2012

CONTENTS

Antonio Paolucci
THE DAVID
THE GLORY AND THE GENIUS
11

A PORTRAIT OF THE DAVID
35

Cristina Bucci
HISTORY OF A MASTERPIECE
71

Chiara Lachi
THE RESTORATION OF THE STATUE
78

Chiara Lachi
THE LIFE OF MICHELANGELO
81

BIBLIOGRAPHY
95

THE DAVID
THE GLORY AND THE GENIUS

David is the greatest, the most dramatic, complex and contradictory character in the Bible. He is the king of Israel, wise lawmaker and victorious general, saint and prophet. He is the author of the Psalms that bear his name and therefore responsible, according to tradition, for the most beautiful poetry in the Old Testament.

David is a "madman of God," and as such we see him leaping and dancing before the Ark of the Alliance in a fit of sublime rapture. Yet David is also the adulterer who sleeps with Bathsheba, and the murderer who sends her husband Uriah into battle to be killed. He is the father who witnesses, heartbroken, the rebellion and tragic death of his son Absalom.

Such a complicated and fascinating personality seems to have been devised expressly to raise multiple and contrasting issues for moral and religious reflection, as well as to provide stimuli for the artistic imagination. However, among the many possible aspects of David, only one appears to have interested the Florentines of the Renaissance. "Their" David was neither the king of Israel nor the prophet, neither the poet nor the adulterer. Their David was the adolescent hero who met the giant Goliath in battle and felled him with a single shot from his sling.

Let us take a look at the passage in the Bible where Samuel evokes the celebrated deed.

The Israelite army, led by King Saul, and the forces of the Philistines are drawn up for the decisive battle. The enemies of the chosen people have a formidable weapon at their disposal: the terrifying giant Goliath, "whose height was six cubits and a span. And he had an helmet of brass upon his head, and he was armed with a coat of mail; and the weight of the coat was five thousand shekels of brass" (1 Sam. 17:4-5). In a fast-moving and gripping sequence resembling the screenplay of a movie, the armored giant comes out and challenges the army of Israel to single combat. Goliath's proposal is simple and brutal. Addressing

the leaders of his opponents, he says "choose you a man for you, and let him come down to me. If he be able to fight with me, and to kill me, then will we be your servants: but if I prevail against him, and kill him, then shall ye be our servants, and serve us" (1 Sam. 17:8-9).

At this point the description of the fight commences. It is worth quoting at length since this brief account has inspired some of the greatest masterpieces in Western art: not just by Michelangelo, but also Donatello and Verrocchio, Gian Lorenzo Bernini and Caravaggio. "And the Philistine came on and drew near unto David; and the man that bare the shield went before him. And when the Philistine looked about, and saw David, he disdained him: for he was but a youth, and ruddy, and of a fair countenance. And the Philistine said unto David, Am I a dog, that thou comest to me with staves? And the Philistine cursed David by his gods. And the Philistine said to David, Come to me, and I will give thy flesh unto the fowls of the air, and to the beasts of the field. Then said David to the Philistine, Thou comest to me with a sword, and with a spear, and with a shield: but I come to thee in the name of the Lord of hosts, the God of the armies of Israel, whom thou hast defied. This day will the Lord deliver thee into mine hand; and I will smite thee, and take thine head from thee; and I will give the carcasses of the host of the Philistines this day unto the fowls of the air, and to the wild beasts of the earth; that all the earth may know that there is a God in Israel. And all this assembly shall know that the Lord saveth not with sword and spear: for the battle is the Lord's, and he will give you into our hands. And it came to pass, when the Philistine arose, and came, and drew nigh to meet David, that David hastened, and ran toward the army to meet the Philistine. And David put his hand in his bag, and took thence a stone, and slang it, and smote the Philistine in his forehead, that the stone sunk into his forehead; and he fell upon his face to the earth. So David prevailed over the Philistine with a sling and with a stone, and smote the Philistine, and slew him; but there was no sword in the hand of David. Therefore David ran, and stood upon the Philistine, and took his sword, and drew it out of the sheath thereof, and slew him, and cut off his head therewith" (1 Sam. 17:41-51).

The story in the Bible is illuminated by two facts that capture our attention and stir our feelings with immediate and absorbing force. The first is the sharp contrast between the two combatants. Goliath is a professional soldier, terrifyingly armed and apparently invincible.

Facing page, Gian Lorenzo Bernini, *David*. Galleria Borghese, Rome

THE GLORY AND THE GENIUS

David, on the contrary, is a delicate and gentle youth, with no experience of fighting and practically unarmed, so that he does indeed seem to merit the derision and contempt of his opponent.

The other element that runs through Samuel's account like an electric shock and that is obvious to all is the presence of God. The outcome of the clash is already decided from the outset because "the Lord saveth not with sword and spear: for the battle is the Lord's," and David is under his protection. The youthful and inexperienced hero is none other than the sling of the Lord. He is merely an instrument in his hands. The shot will hit its target and the giant will be slain whatever the military power of the adversary, for the simple reason that God is invincible and defends his people.

God is invincible and continues to protect his people from tyranny, injustice and external threat just as he protected David in the camp of the Philistines on that day. If the people live in justice and righteousness no enemy will be able to overcome them because God will be on their side. And there will always be a David to act as "the Lord's sling" and punish the godless and the wicked.

The story that Samuel tells must have prompted reflections of this kind in every believer, and everywhere in Christendom, but in Florence it did so with special force and extraordinary results.

The Biblical episode became a political metaphor and allegory of republican liberty for the Florentines.

Renaissance Florence was a wealthy city surrounded by powerful enemies. Its oligarchic government, founded on the supremacy of the great mercantile and financial bourgeoisie, had more than one adversary. The city's institutions were continually under threat. Thus the freedom of the republic appeared an asset as fragile as it was precious. The Florentines intended to defend that asset and there could be no better symbol of their determination than David conquering Goliath.

It is interesting to study the history and iconography of the Florentine images of David that preceded Michelangelo's sculpture. We will find that the representation of David as prophet and king of Israel (still present in the marble sculpture that Andrea Pisano carved around 1340 for one of the niches of Giotto's Tower) gave way to the image of the victo-

Andrea Pisano, *David*. Museo dell'Opera del Duomo, Florence

Antonio del Pollaiuolo, *David*. Staatliche Museen, Berlin

rious youth. Around 1330, in the Baroncelli Chapel in Santa Croce, Taddeo Gaddi painted a fresco of David armed with a sword holding the severed head of Goliath in his left hand.

This painting was the first in a series (which only Michelangelo was to interrupt in revolutionary fashion) that represented the Biblical hero after the duel, triumphant over his defeated and lifeless adversary. In a celebrated scene on the door of the baptistery of San Giovanni called the "Porta del Paradiso," Lorenzo Ghiberti presents us with a battle already over, with the huge corpse of the giant lying on the ground and the young hero in the act of cutting off his head.

In a painting now in the Berlin Staatliche Museen (*c.* 1480), Antonio del Pollaiuolo focuses his attention on the bleeding and grimacing head detached from the body of the vanquished enemy. Pollaiuolo's *David* is a bold and fierce figure, a bundle of taut muscles and nerves, holding Goliath's head between his slightly parted legs, like a soccer player posing for a souvenir photo.

In the painting by Andrea del Castagno in the National Gallery of Washington (*c.* 1450) David has again completed his exploit, for the enemy's severed head is clearly visible in the foreground. But at the same time the painter has chosen to represent, as if in a sequence from a film, the preceding action too: the fatal moment in which the stone hurled from the sling is about to hit its target. And so David is turning on himself in the gesture that Gian Lorenzo Bernini would one day translate into marble in the famous statue in the Galleria Borghese.

The image of David conquering Goliath became extremely popular in 15th-century Florence. It features in illuminated codices, on painted chests, on birthing tables, to the point where it is hard to distinguish between intentionally political messages and purely decorative pretexts.

However, there are three Florentine *Davids* to which special attention should be paid as they are the ones that Michelangelo was surely

THE GLORY AND THE GENIUS

familiar with and that he must have taken into consideration when he was asked to undertake the great enterprise. All three of them are in the Museo Nazionale del Bargello in Florence.

The first and oldest is the work of Donatello: carved from marble, its presence in Palazzo Vecchio is documented from 1416. Donatello's hero gazes at us as if he were posing for a portrait after the victory. His left hand rests jauntily on his hip, the right holds the sling. At the feet of the victorious youth lies Goliath's head. The stone that killed him is clearly visible, still lodged in the center of his forehead. This, the earliest of Donatello's interpretations, is a concentrate of nervous energy, energy that is spiritual rather than physical. David is like a spring ready to be released. The only true precedent for Michelangelo's *David*, along with the *Saint George* formerly in Orsanmichele, is the version that Donatello produced almost a century earlier. Giorgio Vasari grasped this very well when he described Donatello as the precursor of the "divine" Buonarroti.

Donatello's other *David* (a bronze statue dating from around 1435) offers a different and more subtle interpretation of the Bible story. David is very young, almost a boy, and is naked, just as Michelangelo's hero will be naked. Under the victor's foot, laid on top of a wreath of laurel, is the head of his defeated enemy. There is no pride or joy in his triumph. In one hand he holds the stone and in the other the sword, symbols of his triumph, but a hint of sadness seems to be passing over his slightly bowed face, which is shaded by a curious wide-brimmed hat.

The last *David* of the three in the Bargello is the bronze that Andrea del Verrocchio cast for the Medici family in the early 1470s. A recent restoration has considerably improved its definition, bringing out the surviving traces of gold that highlight the hair and the harmonious coating of lustrous patina. It is a masterpiece of quivering vitality. We are now in the cul-

Donatello, *David*, marble statue. Museo Nazionale del Bargello, Florence

Facing page, Donatello, *David*, bronze statue. Museo Nazionale del Bargello, Florence

THE GLORY AND THE GENIUS 17

tural and stylistic climate that will shortly lead to the marvels of Leonardo da Vinci. Rather than moral implications and symbolic references, what seems to fascinate the artist is the physical and psychological spontaneity of the scene represented. The Biblical hero is a young gladiator, muscles rippling beneath his skin, who has just felled his adversary and is now waiting, tense and absorbed, for his well-deserved triumph.

So, while the image of David victorious over Goliath had the significance of a political manifesto in Renaissance Florence, it has to be recognized that never before the years that saw the birth of Michelangelo's sculpture (1501-04) had public proclamation of that message seemed so opportune and even necessary. In effect, at the beginning of the Cinquecento, the freedom of the Florentines appeared to be under serious threat both from within and without. The death of Lorenzo the Magnificent (1492) and the subsequent expulsion of the Medici family (1494) had shattered the fragile balance of power on the Italian peninsula. The consequences had been the invasion of Italy by King Charles VIII of France and the short-lived adventure of Duke Valentino Borgia, who devastated the Marche and Romagna with his army of mercenaries, coming close to Florence itself, with the aim of building a vast kingdom on the ruins of the seignories. The Medici, temporarily exiled from the city but far from defeated, maneuvered to regain power, while domestic dissidence gelled around the memory of Girolamo Savonarola (burned at the stake in 1498) and his utopian ideas imbued with political radicalism and religious fundamentalism.

The chronicles tell us that the erection of Michelangelo's statue in the square in front of Palazzo Vecchio, i.e. in the place most representative of civic authority, was the result of a lively debate and a majority decision taken on January 25 1504 by a commission made up of numerous artists, including some of the best known and most admired: Piero di Cosimo, Perugino, Leonardo da Vinci, Botticelli, Filippino Lippi, Cosimo Rosselli and Andrea della Robbia. We know that the decision was opposed and that several of the most authoritative members of the commission (Leonardo da Vinci in particular) preferred a less prominent location. It is also likely that Michelangelo did everything he could to ensure that his masterpiece was placed in the more eminent position, which it occupied up until 1873. However, I believe that the Gonfalonier of Justice (Chief Magistrate), Pier Soderini, the man who had prized the sculpture away from the Vestry Board of Santa Maria del

Facing page,
Andrea del Verrocchio,
David.
Museo Nazionale del Bargello,
Florence

Fiore, which had originally commissioned it, was very pleased with the decision reached. What politically more effective location could be imagined than in front of Palazzo Vecchio, the city's most symbolic setting? Michelangelo's *David* had to convey both a sense of calm and of strength. David could not be a delicate adolescent but a young man at the height of his physical vigor. He had to look grand and majestic, to resemble Hercules, the epitome of invincible and virtuous might. The citizens should see him as a colossus and a giant, for the statue was intended to be a visible emblem of the power of the republic, whose strength derived from the fact that God was watching over it. All these values and meanings, implicit in the sculpture, were multiplied and enhanced and made immediately perceptible by its erection in front of the entrance to Palazzo Vecchio.

Among the most celebrated works of art in the world (those ten or fifteen that everyone knows), none is more "polysemous," i.e. possessing multiple meanings, than Michelangelo's *David*.

With regard to the iconographic significance becoming a political metaphor, I do not know how many of the visitors who enter the Galleria dell'Accademia every year (over one million two hundred thousand of them) are capable of grasping the symbolic meaning of the *David* by linking the image to the history of early 16th-century Florence. But everyone understands that this sculpture conveys universal values of dignity, justice and liberty. So its original significance, however blurred and indistinct, has not been wholly lost.

The other meaning that the statue is still able to transmit stems from a critical-aesthetic judgment. It was first put forward by Giorgio Vasari and opinion has not changed in the last five centuries. This, says Vasari, is the statue of victory. With his *David,* Michelangelo outstripped the ancients, eclipsing both Phidias and Polyclitus. The sculpture the Florentines inaugurated on September 8, 1504 exhausted the very possibilities of the statue. "To be sure, anyone who has seen Michelangelo's *David* has no need to see anything else by any other sculptor, living or dead," as the historian from Arezzo put it; in other words: *David* is the most beautiful statue in the world, no one could produce anything better, and you have to come and see it for yourself. The extent to which that judgment was correct is demonstrated by the permanent lines of visitors outside the Galleria dell'Accademia.

In reality Giorgio Vasari is saying something even more important.

Facing page, marble copy of the *David* in front of Palazzo Vecchio, Florence

He is claiming that Michelangelo's *David* is the first "modern" statue, that the sculptors of antiquity have been surpassed and defeated, that "our" history of art starts from here, from the Colossus that the Florentines saw standing in all its glory before Palazzo Vecchio on September 8 of the year of Our Lord 1504. This, in essence, is what Vasari is trying to say.

Why such a peremptory claim and yet, in many ways, such a true one? Where does the modernity of the *David* lie, its "discontinuity" with respect to what came before, the fact that it is, in a certain sense, an avant-garde work? I believe that the modernity of the *David* consists in the fact that, for the first time, spiritual values (thought, intellect, will, spirit, idea) were made the absolute, even exclusive protagonists of the artistic representation. It may seem strange to make a claim of this kind for a work whose subject is the splendid physicality of a standing male nude: never before represented on such a grand scale and with so much realism. And yet an examination of the sculpture that goes beyond the superficial will convince us that this is the right interpretation if we want to grasp the revolutionary innovation of Michelangelo's masterpiece. Let us consider the iconography.

David – as we have seen in the numerous examples cited above – had always been represented in relation to his opponent and, usually, at the end of his victorious duel, with the severed head of his enemy deposited as a macabre trophy at his feet. Michelangelo ignores the established conventions and invents another David, different from the familiar images. His hero is not depicted immediately prior to the combat, for there is no stone in his right hand, as is often mistakenly claimed, but only the grip of the sling. Nor is he shown after the combat because the head of his vanquished enemy is not lying at his feet, as required by iconographic convention.

David is about to carry out the deed of which the Bible speaks. He is ready to fight. His physical and mental concentration has reached a climax. The whole of his body is in tension, the muscles that wrap his limbs like a splendid and powerful sheath are a lethal machine of restrained energy, ready to be unleashed. The abnormally large right hand, rippling with nerves, grips the end of the sling which, carried over his left shoulder, will launch the fatal blow.

Nothing tells us, however, that the duel is about to commence. It may start at any moment or not for a long time yet, and in any case

David – vigilant, absorbed, his muscles, will, intellect and heart on the alert – is always in that state. He is always ready for combat and has never let down his guard.

So it is correct to say that Michelangelo's *David* is not represented, but rather "is." He is the gladiator of Israel whom God protects, but at the same time he "is" the freedom and dignity of all men who must always be ready to oppose tyranny and injustice. David is a Florentine and he is Everyman. He is of 1504 and he is of all time. This statue speaks of a hero of the Bible who defeated Evil. But – by a symbolic transference – he also alludes to the Evil of today. And it says, this statue, that it is Man's inescapable duty to confront Goliath with courage: the "monster" Goliath who surfaces in one way or another in every period of history to obstruct the path of liberty and civilization.

Never before had the ideal and spiritual values that I have sought to recapitulate here dominated a work of art with such peremptory force. This is why Giorgio Vasari was right when he asserted that this was the first modern statue.

The other new iconographic feature (charged in this case, too, with ideological and spiritual meanings of extraordinary intensity and clarity) concerns the total nudity of the Biblical hero. There can be no doubt that Michelangelo, with his perfect understanding of human anatomy (as he had demonstrated in his representation of Christ's body draped over his Mother's knees in the *Pietà* in St. Peter's, and in the *Bacchus* now in the Bargello), intended to mount a challenge to the great tradition of Greco-Roman statuary (exemplified in his day by the *Dioscuri* uncovered on Montecavallo), surpassing it in the very area in which it had historically excelled, the naturalistic representation of the standing male nude. Vasari was the first to declare Buonarroti the winner of the contest, and generations of historians and critics have shared his opinion. But for Michelangelo the Christian, the *David's* nudity had another, essentially religious significance.

David is naked like the Hercules of myth. He is totally naked, without even the footwear and headgear in which Donatello had dressed his bronze hero. It is a nudity

Michelangelo, *Bacchus*. Museo Nazionale del Bargello, Florence

that takes to its logical consequences the Biblical text, which speaks of a practically defenseless David who refuses armor and sword and goes into combat without fear because he is certain of divine protection.

For the man who has placed himself in the hands of God the force of arms is irrelevant, the outward signs of power and rank are meaningless. So why not represent the hero that the Lord has chosen as his instrument completely naked? All men who set out to oppose Evil, who fight for Justice and Freedom, carry with them the power of omnipotent God. Protected by the Almighty, all they need to prevail is their naked humanity. Michelangelo's sculpture aims to convey not only civil and patriotic values, but also faith in Providence and awareness of the presence of God in history: grand ideas that cry out for concrete expression.

A work of art in which forms are used to communicate an idea is a "conceptual" work of art. It is, therefore, a *modern* work of art. The innovation and thus the "discontinuity" of the *David* with respect to the models of the past is so marked that on the five hundredth anniversary of the unveiling of the statue, in the fall of 2004, an exhibition (*Forms for the David*) was staged in the Galleria dell'Accademia bringing together five great artists of our own day: George Baselitz, Luciano Fabro, Jannis Kounellis, Robert Morris and Thomas Struth. The works of these artists, described by some as "provocative" or even "sacrilegious," serve to demonstrate the "discontinuity" of contemporary figurative art with regard to the forms of the past. They help us to understand the role played five centuries ago by Michelangelo's *David*, it too being both "discontinuous" with respect to the past and the product of an intellectual and formal experimentation destined to make it, from then on, a lodestar for artists.

The contemporary works of art put on display in the home of the *David* set out to show that modernity in all its innovative and transgressive forms has its roots in Buonarroti's masterpiece, owing a greater debt to Michelangelo than to anyone else.

We have said that the *David* is charged with meanings that are still to some extent comprehensible today. However, there is one that overshadows all the others since, thanks to its impact on popular imagination, it is absolutely the most important. It is the sense of what I will call "divinization," meaning the divinization of Michelangelo in the history of the arts and – as part of that phenomenon and indeed its cul-

The *Prisoners*, with the *David* in the background, as they appeared in the late 1960s

mination – the divinization of the statue that used to stand in front of Palazzo Vecchio and now in the Galleria dell'Accademia.

The "Sublime" Michelangelo: it is almost impossible for us to shrug off the weight of a critical judgment that has intimidated and conditioned people for centuries. The concept of Michelangelo's *sublimità* (or his *terribilità* or *divinità*, no less peremptory variants of this "sublimity") has been firmly attached to his name since the time of Ascanio Condivi and Giorgio Vasari; since, that is, the accounts of his contemporaries.

The biography of Michelangelo in Vasari's *Lives* begins: "[…] the great Ruler of Heaven looked down and […] resolved […] to send to earth a genius universal in each art, to show single-handed the perfection of line and shadow, and who should give relief to his paintings, show a sound judgment in sculpture […]. He further endowed him with true moral philosophy and a sweet poetic spirit, so that the world should marvel at the singular eminence of his life and works and all his actions, seeming rather divine than earthly."

So Vasari, Michelangelo's contemporary, described him as "rather divine than earthly." The process of divinization had already taken place. For Vasari the birth of Michelangelo was no common human

THE GLORY AND THE GENIUS

birth but an "epiphany," a manifestation of the divine. The emergence of his style was the epoch-making event that concluded – at the peak of a perfection unsurpassed and unsurpassable ever since – the age-old labor of the arts.

No different was the attitude of Ascanio Condivi, the favorite pupil in whom admiration and reverence seem to be veiled and softened by feelings of love. Here is how he begins his *Life*: "Since the time when the Lord God, by his singular beneficence, made me worthy no longer just of the presence (into which I would barely have hoped to be able to come) but of the love, the conversation and the close familiarity of Michelangelo Buonarroti, unique painter and sculptor …". Condivi describes his intimacy with the great artist in tones of mystical experience, speaking of it as an ineffable privilege and transfiguring it into a world of higher sentiments and values.

Right from the outset, therefore, the myth of Michelangelo, was built around the concepts of uniqueness, of awesomeness, of "otherness."

It is worth including a very brief critical anthology: "I am such a total enthusiast of Michelangelo that not even Nature satisfies me any more after him, not being able to see her with eyes as great as his" (Goethe, *Italian Journey*); "The only feeling that divinity can inspire in frail mortals is terror; and Michelangelo seems to have been born for the express purpose of instilling this fear into their souls" (Stendhal, *Promenades dans Rome*); "From the very first moment Michelangelo was a complete personality; almost frightening in his unilaterality" (Heinrich Wölfflin).

The process of exaltation has continued right down to the literary inventions, biographies and movies of our own day: Michelangelo as a "God" or "Titan." Thus a critical idea born with Vasari and Condivi, and skillfully nurtured by the artist himself in his own lifetime through his thought processes and literary influences, has survived into our own time, influencing the thoughts and behavior of millions of people and rendering difficult, in the last analysis, a correct historical and critical understanding of the artist. Today, for the public all over the world, Michelangelo is a "fatal attraction." No other artist of the past (with the sole exception of Leonardo) has earned such vast, uncritical and unconditional appreciation. And it is certainly no coincidence that in recent years Michelangelo's most iconic sculptures (the *Pietà* in St. Peter's, the *David* in the Accademia) have come under attack from madmen. In a sense such episodes are the pathological aspect of Myth. The attraction for the artist is reversed in its dark mirror. The roots of all this, if we think about it carefully, lie in the critical interpretation that has been made of Michelangelo throughout history.

The removal of the *David* from Piazza della Signoria in 1873 and its transfer to the Accademia because of its precarious state of preservation represents the climax – as has been pointed out – of the process of divinization initiated with Giorgio Vasari's biography. Once the sculpture had been moved to the Accademia, the architect Emilio De Fabris devised a setting for it that is a genuine masterpiece of celebratory presentation. The *David* was placed on a pedestal at the center of a vaulted exedra with an apse, almost as if it were the Eucharistic altar of a Catholic church. Flooded with light from the skylight above, isolated in its disquieting beauty and almost transported outside time and history, the Biblical prophet, once the symbol of republican freedoms, became the modern totem of the universal imagery of tourism: the most beautiful statue in the world, the most beautiful man in the world.

The last, brilliant act of mythicizing the *David* was carried out by Corrado Ricci in 1909. The statue, standing by itself in De Fabris's tribune, needed a suitable context. What was required was a majestic prelude that would lead the visitor to contemplation of the masterpiece. For this reason Ricci, head of the Monuments and Fine Arts Service, took from the Grotta del Buontalenti in the Boboli Gardens the *Prisoners* that Michelangelo had carved for the tomb of Julius II but left unfinished, which Mannerist taste had transformed into "rustic" décor, and placed them, along with the also incomplete statue of *Saint Matthew* intended for Santa Maria del Fiore, to the right and left of the nave leading to the tribune. A sort of sublime guard of honor.

Michelangelo, *Pietà*. St. Peter's, Vatican

Following De Fabris's creation of the tribune, completed by Ricci's intervention, the *David* has undergone a sort of secular consecration. It is under this predominant aspect – an aspect that obscures the historical and symbolic ones I have tried to define above – that the majority of the people who come from all over the world to visit the Galleria dell'Accademia now see it.

Just how great is the halo of myth surrounding the *David* became apparent on the occasion of its recent restoration. Rather than a "restoration," in fact, it was an extremely gentle cleaning carried out with substances so innocuous (distilled water and cellulose) that they could be used to wash the skin of a baby. In reality, behind this mild cleaning, behind a restoration that has been described as "invisible," lay ten years of scientific analysis by dozens of professionals and specialists of every aspect (historical, documentary, physical, structural) of the sculpture. All was carried out under an umbrella of security provided by the Opificio delle Pietre Dure in Florence, the Centro Nazionale delle Ricerche Beni Culturali and numerous Italian and foreign university institutions: from the Department of Physics at Milan Polytechnic to Stanford University, from the E.N.E.A. in Rome to the Department of Chemical Sciences at the University of Catania. The intervention could not have been so minimal had it not been backed up by technical and scientific monitoring of this importance and caliber.

But the world's media were not interested in the formidable deployment of technical and scientific expertise that had preceded and accompanied the cleaning. What interested (and frightened) them was the fact that someone should dare to touch the skin of *David*. This raised the level of emotion and anxiety to fever pitch. What if the cleaning were to leave us with a *David* different from the one that people remembered, if the "immaterial" patina (i.e. the manner in which we are accustomed to see it) of that all too famous sculpture were to be in some way violated or diminished or obscured?

Well, nothing of the kind occurred this time. No one will be able to say (as often happens at the conclusion of such a project) "it was better before." The *David* is how we have always seen it. Its color has not changed. Only those who are old hands, thoroughly familiar with the "skin" of the celebrated statue through long experience and habit, will notice that certain unappealing aesthetic irregularities are no longer there, that the deposits of ingrained dirt have dissolved, that the whole thing today looks more fluid, more coherent, more harmonious. The *David* is what it has always been. The sculpture, caressed, worn and rendered precious by its five hundred years of existence, has preserved intact its modulations of color, the wearing of its surface, the marks of time, in a word the appearance that history has given it.

The result is exactly what we wanted. We wanted the people who come to the Accademia not to realize that the *David* has been restored, that the male anatomy admired by millions of tourists has been subjected to a very light cleaning. A restoration that does not seem to be a restoration is always the best restoration. In the *David's* case that type of "invisible" intervention was particularly necessary precisely because of the aura of myth in which the sculpture is cloaked. So it was right to protect it from even the slightest alteration that might disappoint the memory and expectations of the public.

There is another aspect of the *David* that needs to be examined and understood: the representation and indeed the glorification of male beauty.

When Michelangelo finished carving the sculpture he was still in his twenties. He was at the peak of a stylistic phase (the first of many that he passed through over the course of his very long life) that is called "classicism". During this period he pursued the Platonic ideal of pure beauty, representing it through naturalistic forms that were perfectly finished and polished, mimicking visible reality. He had asserted this aesthetic ideal several years earlier (1499) with the *Pietà* in St. Peter's, a work that astonished the world and that still has the look of a flawless gem: the gleaming splendor of the flesh, the prodigy of the drapery handled with boundless skill, the supreme and luminous perfection of the finish, the lunar pallor of the Virgin's unforgettable face. In the *Pietà* in St. Peter's the "beauty of the soul" (the 16th-century equivalent of the concept of grace) shines from every detail of the modeling. It is still a long way from the period of the "*non finito*," of his inability to be "satisfied" with his work: the time when the *idea* would appear so great to the artist that he found it to some extent inexpressible, thereby justifying his failure to conclude the process of execution and even preventing him from doing so.

Michelangelo, *Rondanini Pietà*. Castello Sforzesco, Milan

This reflection on Buonarroti's artistic history, on the course of his mental and stylistic development, is important as it allows us to grasp the specific character of the *David* more clearly.

In fact it is not possible to understand the famous statue fully without taking into account the process of Buonarroti's intellectual and therefore artistic growth, without giving it its place in "his" history.

Between the statue unveiled in front of the entrance of Palazzo Vecchio in 1504 and the *Rondanini Pietà* now in Milan's Museo del Castello Sforzesco, the sculpture on which the ninety-year-old Michelangelo was still working in February 1564, shortly before his death (according to his pupil Daniele da Volterra), sixty years would go by: a significant lapse of historical time, over which decisive changes can take place. Rarely, however, in the history of the human race, has such a radical shift taken place as the one that affected Italy and Europe between the beginning and the middle of the 16th century. In those crucial decades, with the Lutheran Reformation and religious conflicts, the spiritual unity of the West was shattered forever. The wars for control of Italy between the great European powers led to the Sack of Rome (1527) and the bloody suppression of Florentine liberty with the siege of 1530, restoring Medici rule with the backing of Spanish pikes. The peninsula became a battleground for the armies of France and Spain. The independence of cities and dynasties waned. Against a background of general impoverishment, the power of the bourgeoisie diminished while feudal ideologies and customs were revived. At the same time the new religious climate fostered anxiety and dissent among the intellectual classes and prompted a vigorous surge of self-criticism and spiritual renewal in the Catholic Church, only to be followed, with the Council of Trent (1545-65) and the so-called Counter-Reformation, by the imposition of repressive and strict measures that were to have a deep influence on culture and modes of artistic expression.

An equally profound mutation took place in the world of the figurative arts over that decisive sixty-year period. While the 16th century seemed to have been born under the sign of grace, equilibrium and harmony, with a widespread optimism permeating the imagery of artists and writers, the "subtle crest of classicism," to use Wölfflin's celebrated phrase, was soon passed and swept away by the emergence of new expressive requirements.

The age of the classical ideal that had been epitomized by Raphael (who died in 1520) evolved into the Mannerist period. The declared objective of the art of that time was to accentuate difficulties, rarities and diversities, leading in many cases to a transcendence of the real elements of nature in order to permit their symbolic interpretation and metaphorical transfiguration. The results, with different emphases in relation to psychological dispositions and cultural ambiences, were often forms of aestheticism, individualism and mysticism. According to the theorists of the age of Mannerism, what mattered was not the imitation of nature but its ideal transcendence. Thus the guide to be followed became "the inner image," cherished in the heart and controlled by the mind.

The chief architect of the intellectual and artistic evolution that I have attempted to summarize here was, in the 16th century, Michelangelo Buonarroti. As far as the history of the figurative arts in Italy and Europe is concerned, the Cinquecento was dominated, directly or indirectly, by Michelangelo.

All this is intended to show that there are several profoundly different phases in the work of the man who shaped the century. So it would be reductive to look at the *David* in isolation from all that came after: an after which is in a certain sense anticipated and prefigured in the sculpture now in the Accademia. It is no accident that Vasari argued that Modernity, with its continual transformations, with its unquenchable thirst for intellectual research and formal experimentation, began with that very statue.

If we examine the whole body of Buonarroti's work with a degree of detachment, the impression we receive is of a vast and turbulent river that embraces all the utopian ideas, spiritual tensions, dramas and hopes of the century in its course, and translates them into images of majesty and power.

There is a young Michelangelo who shares the optimistic ideals and unblemished formal splendor of the early Renaissance (this is the time of the *Bacchus* in the Bargello, the *Pietà* in St. Peter's and the *David* in the Accademia). There is the Michelangelo of his full maturity who seems to be taking on the Universe and History in a "hand-to-hand" fight (the *Moses* and the *Prisoners* for Julius II's tomb, the *Sistine Chapel*). And finally there is the Michelangelo of the final years, those of spiritual anguish and the ultimate rarefaction of style (the *Pauline Chapel*, the *Pietà* in Santa Maria del Fiore, the *Rondanini Pietà*).

So let us look at the *David* against the backdrop of history. It is something that visitors to the Accademia do not usually do, so effective has the process of divinization been in transforming it into an object of uncritical contemplation, outside and above time.

Let us set the *David* in its history: the history of the city for which it was created, the artistic history of its creator (thinking of all that had come before but also everything that followed, the *Prisoners* struggling to break free from the oppression of matter, the cataclysmic nudes of the *Last Judgment*, the desolate gloom of the last *Pietà*) and the history of a man called Michelangelo Buonarroti who was twenty-nine years old at the time when his masterpiece was erected in Piazza della Signoria.

Once again we must turn to Giorgio Vasari. The historian from Arezzo has in a certain sense been the official critic of Michelangelo because it was he who constructed his image and set the seal on his fame, but he was also a confidant and friend of the great artist, writing about the *David* as quoted above. He says that it is the statue of victory because the ancients have finally been surpassed, that the history of modern art starts from here. It is the judgment of a great historian, of someone who understands the evolution of the arts over time, who knows how to select and appraise works and their authors and to pick out, in history, the watersheds, the moments of discontinuity and progress. But Vasari is also able to penetrate the work of art with the instruments of aesthetic sensibility and emotional and psychological empathy. He looks at the sculpture, caressing it with his gaze and praising its elegance and the accuracy of its anatomy, the skill and "grace" of the modeling and the way that "the legs are finely turned, the slender flanks divine." He expresses his wonder at "the graceful pose unequalled."

The sculpture that appears to be (and in effect is) an unrivaled celebration of athletic male virility also merits comments on the "grace" of the "pose," the flanks so beautiful and "slender" that they are described as "divine." Is there not a contradiction, an ambiguity in this line of judgment? There certainly is, but it is the same contradiction, the same ambiguity, as guided Michelangelo when he sculpted his *David*.

With the sensitivity that only great critics possess, Giorgio Vasari has carried out a sort of transference. He has put himself in Michelangelo's shoes and looked at the statue with the same "loving gaze" as did the young Buonarroti when he conceived and realized his masterpiece.

David is the victorious hero, he is the champion of Florentine freedom, he is the sling of the Lord, he is the symbol of the Virtue that God protects and that no enemy will ever be able to overcome. But the *David* is also "the affectionate fantasy that made art an idol and sovereign to me," as Michelangelo himself would admit in a famous sonnet written in old age. The *David* is the virile beauty who claims his rights and who in this period of his life and his style occupies and dominates the artist's mind and guides his hands, like an "idol," like a "sovereign."

The thing that Giorgio Vasari had clearly sensed, and that every visitor to the Accademia is more or less aware of, is Michelangelo's homosexuality. His was a homosexuality transfigured and sublimated by intellectual and philosophical motivations, but this does not mean that we feel its presence any less.

In a celebrated sonnet written for Tommaso de' Cavalieri Michelangelo describes the state of ecstasy induced by the beauty of his young friend.

> "With your fair eyes a charming light I see,
>   For which my own blind eyes would peer in vain;
>   Stayed by your feet the burden I sustain
>   Which my lame feet find all too strong for me;
> Wingless upon your pinions forth I fly;
>   Heavenward your spirit stirreth me to strain;
>   E'en as you will, I blush and blanch again,
>   Freeze in the sun, burn 'neath a frosty sky.
> Your will includes and is the lord of mine;
>   Life to my thoughts within your heart is given;
>   My words begin to breathe upon your breath:
> Like to the moon am I, that cannot shine
>   Alone; for lo! our eyes see nought in heaven
>   Save what the living sun illumineth."

The lover sees with the eyes of the beloved, thinks with his thoughts, walks with his feet, wishes to be wherever he is, effaces himself in his will. This is how Michelangelo Buonarroti speaks of Tommaso de' Cavalieri, and in doing so seems to have entered into Roland Barthes's *A Lover's Discourse.*

Also dedicated to Cavalieri is the charcoal drawing of the *Rape of Ganymede,* now in the Fogg Art Museum, Cambridge (Mass.). The myth of Ganymede, carried to heaven by Jupiter's eagle, is a recurring motif of the literary and artistic imagery of the Italian Renaissance. Usually it was given a neoplatonic interpretation, in which the beautiful youth transported to Olympus by the sacred bird symbolized the human soul and its process of elevation through love and understanding. Michelangelo draws on this official allegorical interpretation, but anyone familiar with that sublime image knows very well that the erotic impulse has rarely been represented with such intensity, with the eagle's talons gripping with vehement passion the naked body of the handsome youth, who surrenders to his fate in a sort of complicit languor.

In the *David* the amorous cult of male beauty (*vagheggiamento* or "longing" as it was called in the old treatises) reached its height and produces in the observer that ambiguous admiration which is not the least of the reasons for its fascination. It is not hard to understand why the most beautiful man in the world, the perfect symbol of heterosexual virility, is also a gay icon. It is from this perspective that he has been evoked by such great contemporary artists as Andy Warhol.

Thus the *David* can also be said to be a symbol of ambiguity, remembering, however, that ambiguity, plurality, ambivalence, are distinctive features of modernity, as Giorgio Vasari clearly grasped when he dated the beginning of "our" history of art from that sculpture.

We could also say, paradoxically, that the real *David* does not exist, contradicted as it is by its sublime ambiguity, obscured and distorted by its overexposure in the mass media to the point where everyone can make a *David* all of his or her own, molding it out of memories, feelings, experiences of life, philosophical and religious ideals.

These are legitimate and justified reflections if we bear in mind the fact that the sculpture has entered the hearts and minds of millions of people of the most diverse origin, culture and level of education. One thing is certain, however. The marble Giant who stands in the Galleria dell'Accademia and whom the Florentines first saw gleaming in the sun of their square one September day five centuries ago is still young and marvelously up to date. He still astonishes, disturbs and moves us.

Antonio Paolucci

A PORTRAIT OF THE DAVID

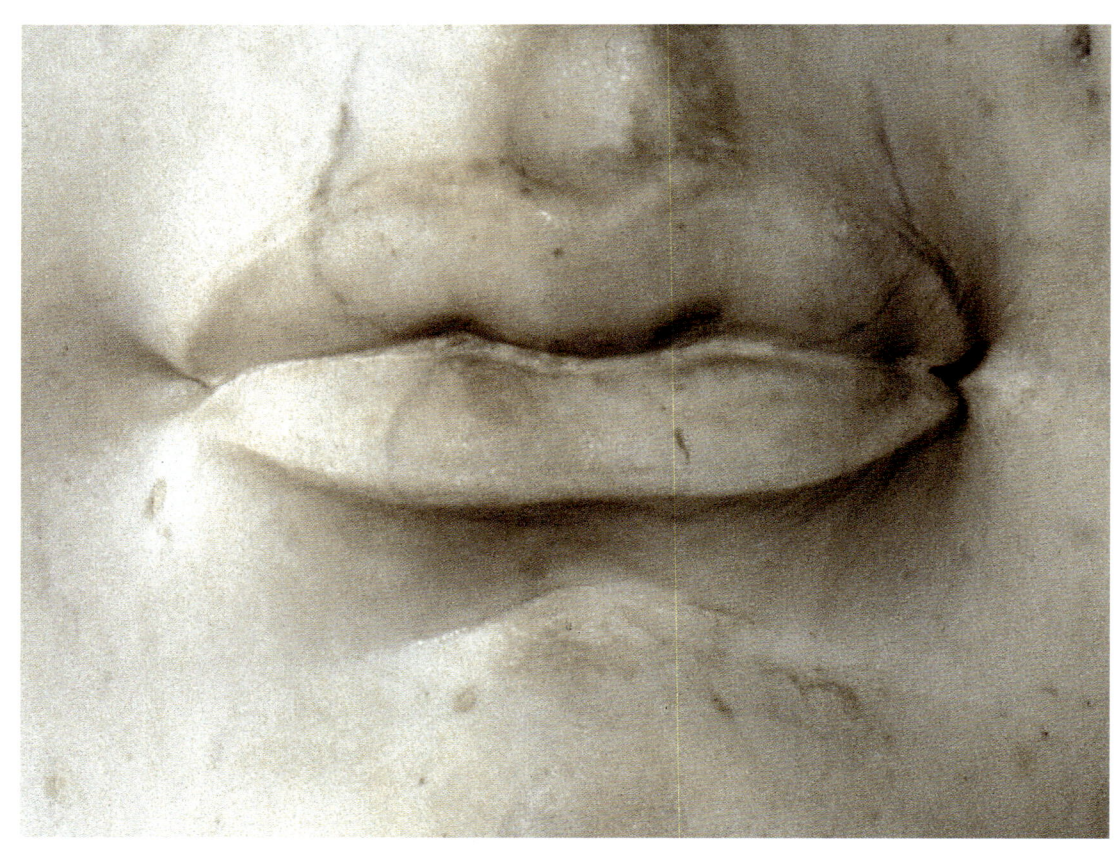

48　A PORTRAIT OF THE DAVID

A PORTRAIT OF THE DAVID

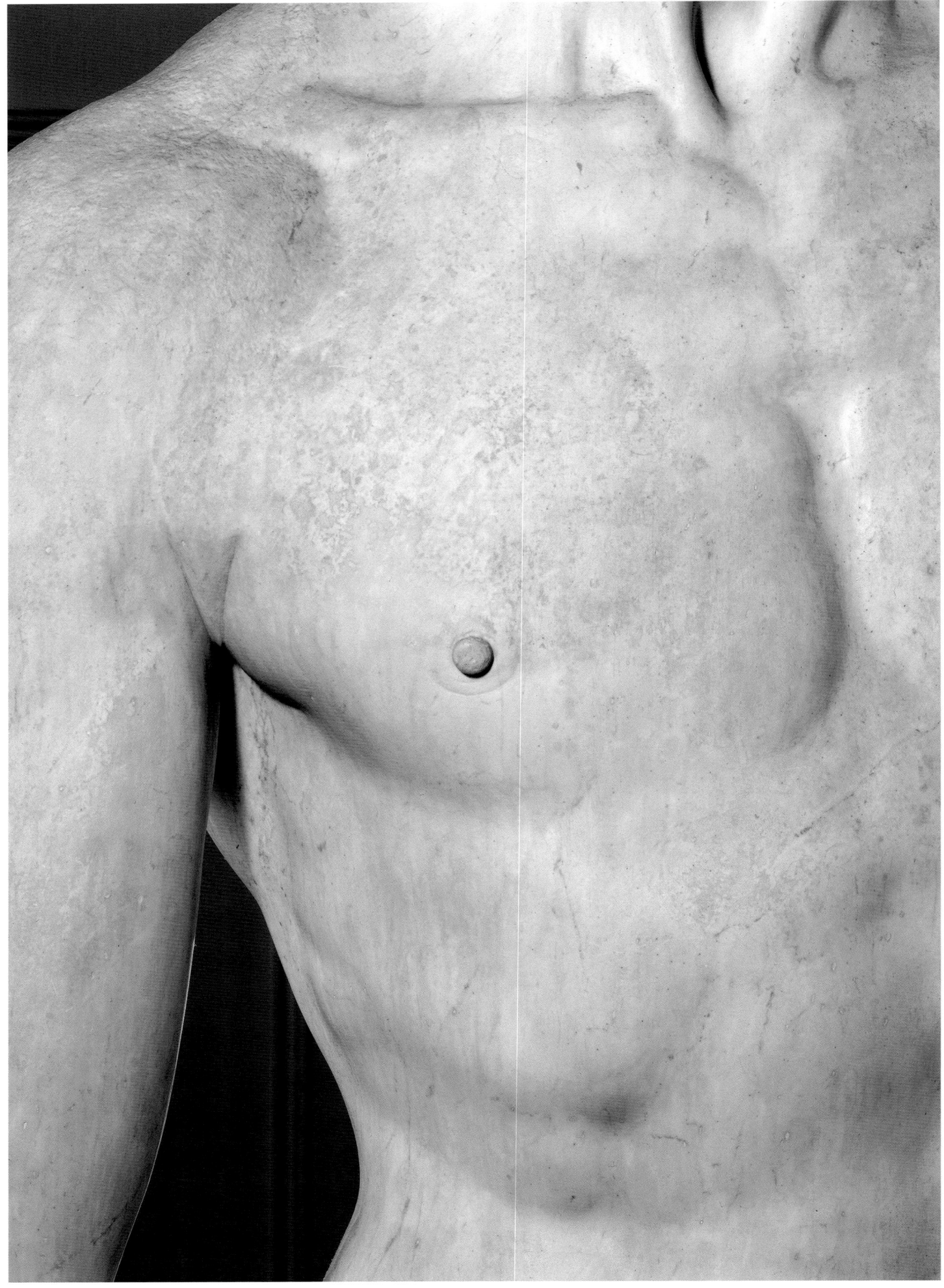

50   A PORTRAIT OF THE DAVID

52 A PORTRAIT OF THE DAVID

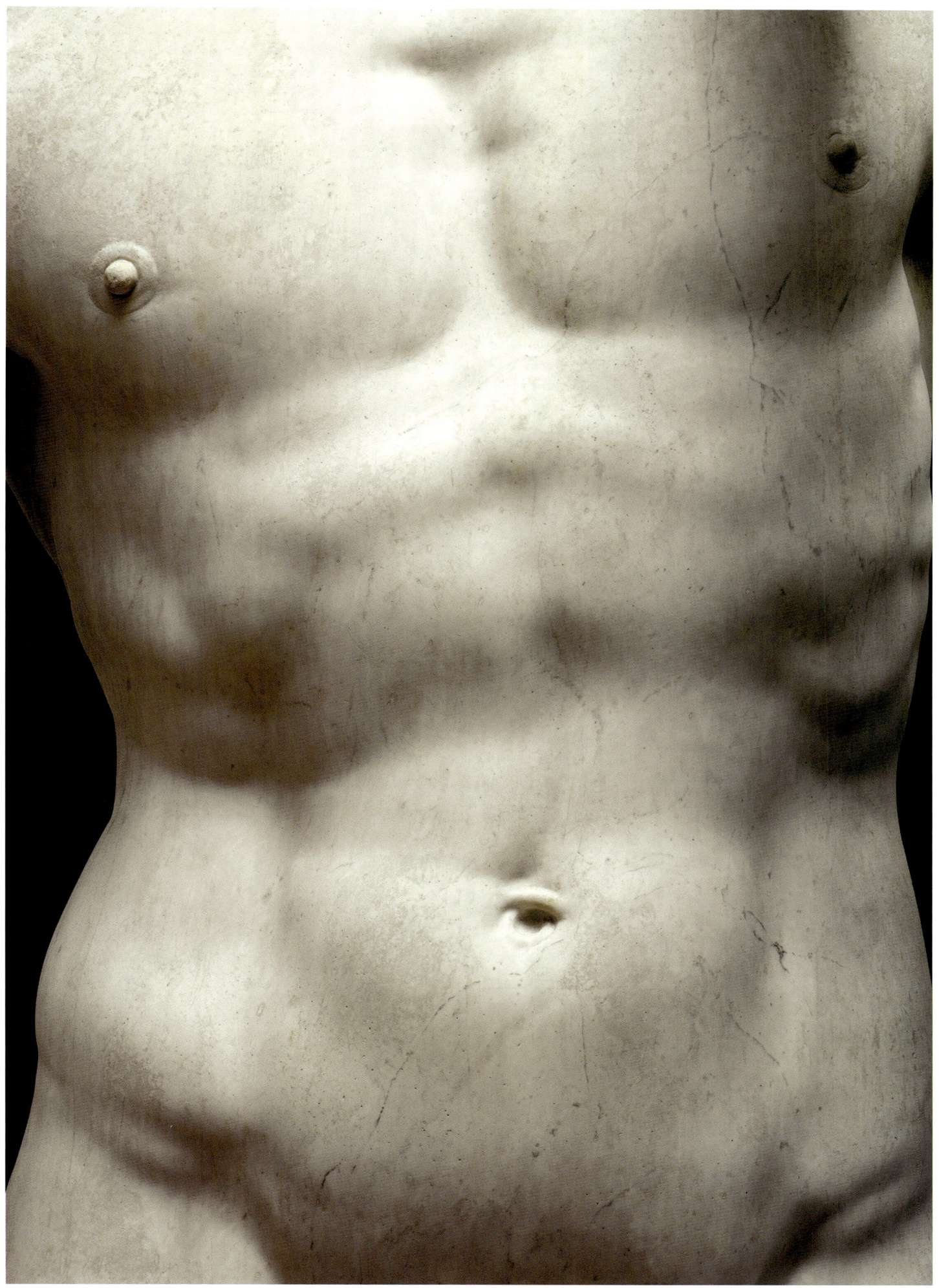

A PORTRAIT OF THE DAVID

58 A PORTRAIT OF THE DAVID

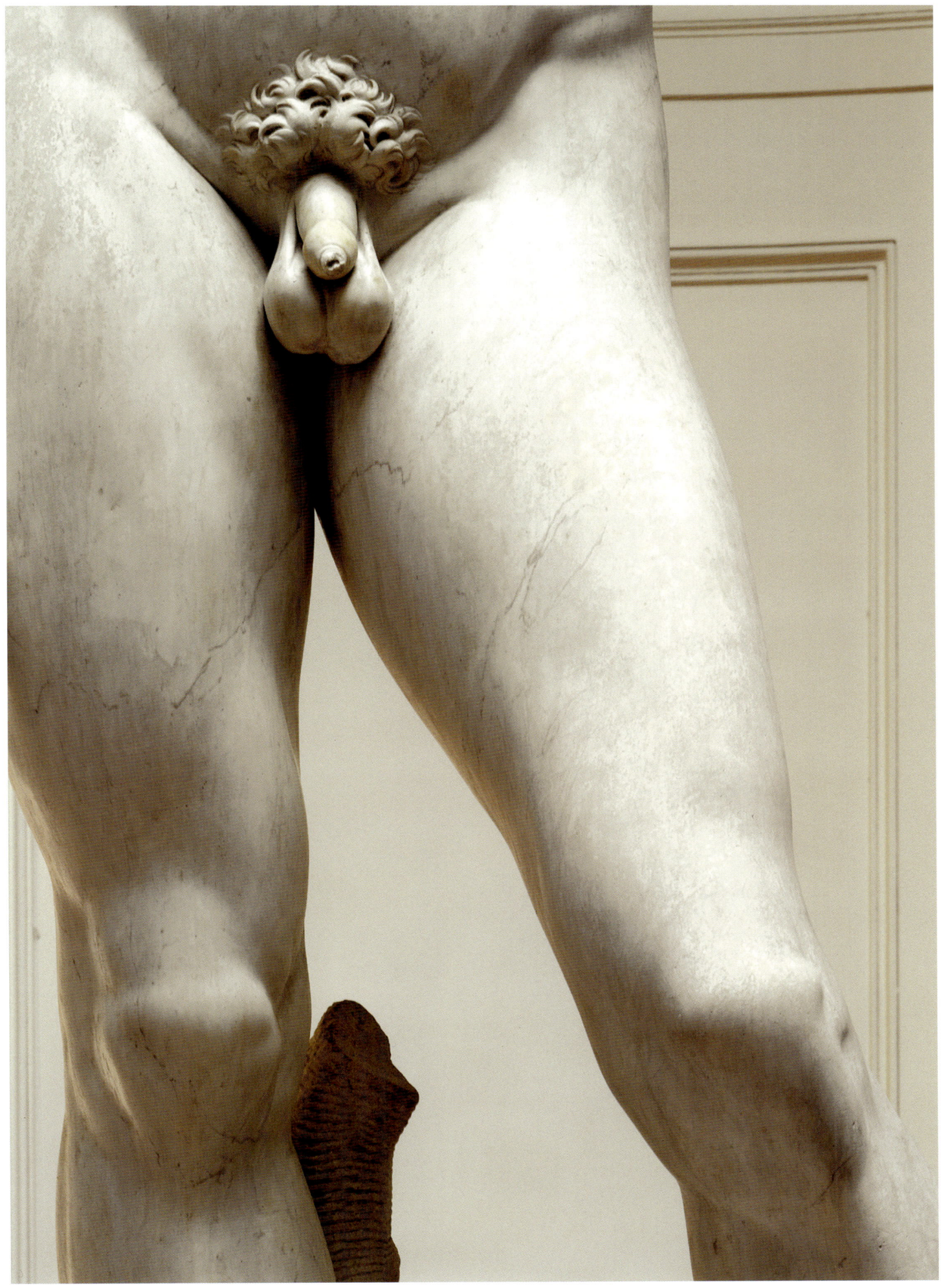

A PORTRAIT OF THE DAVID

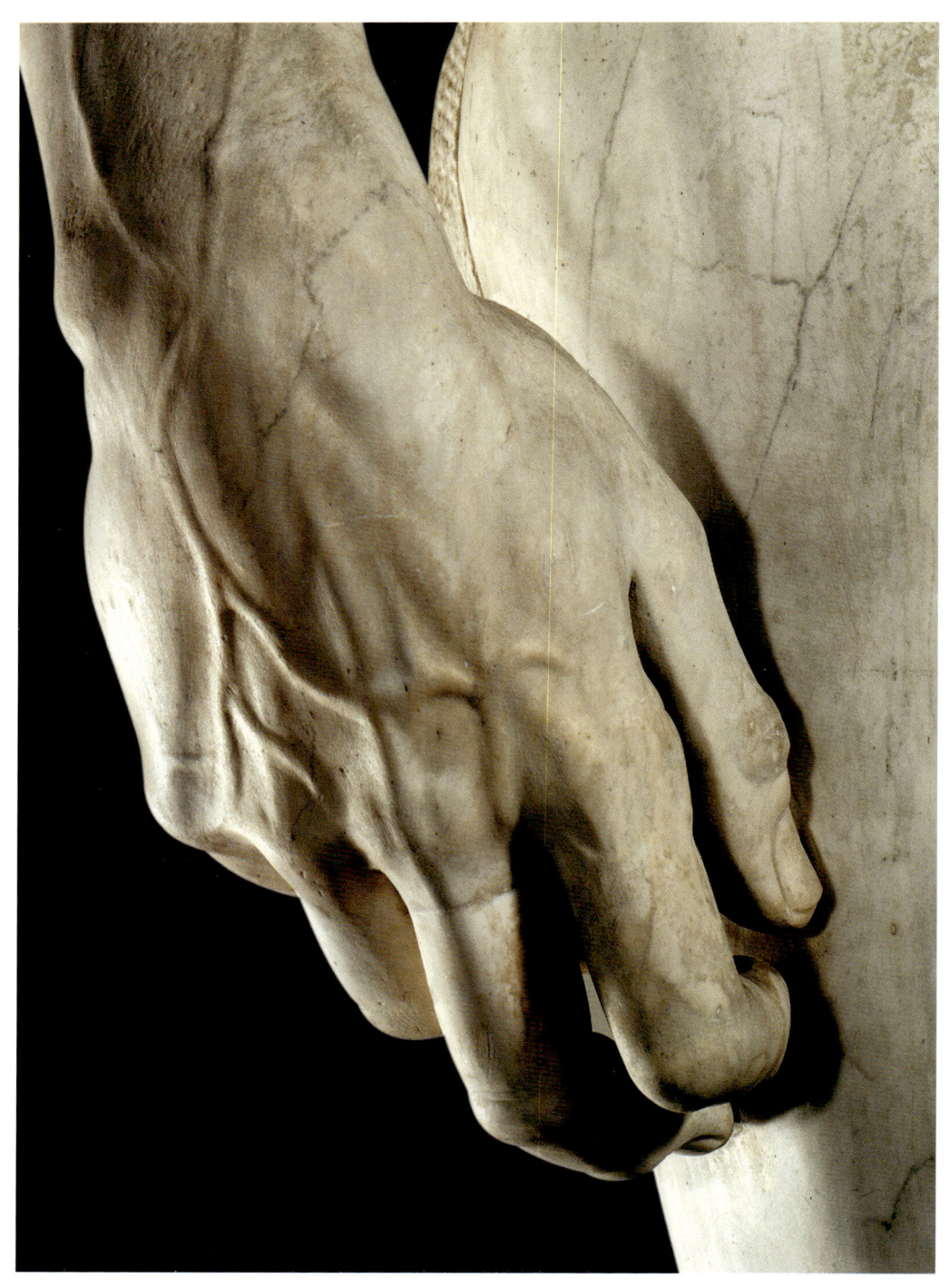

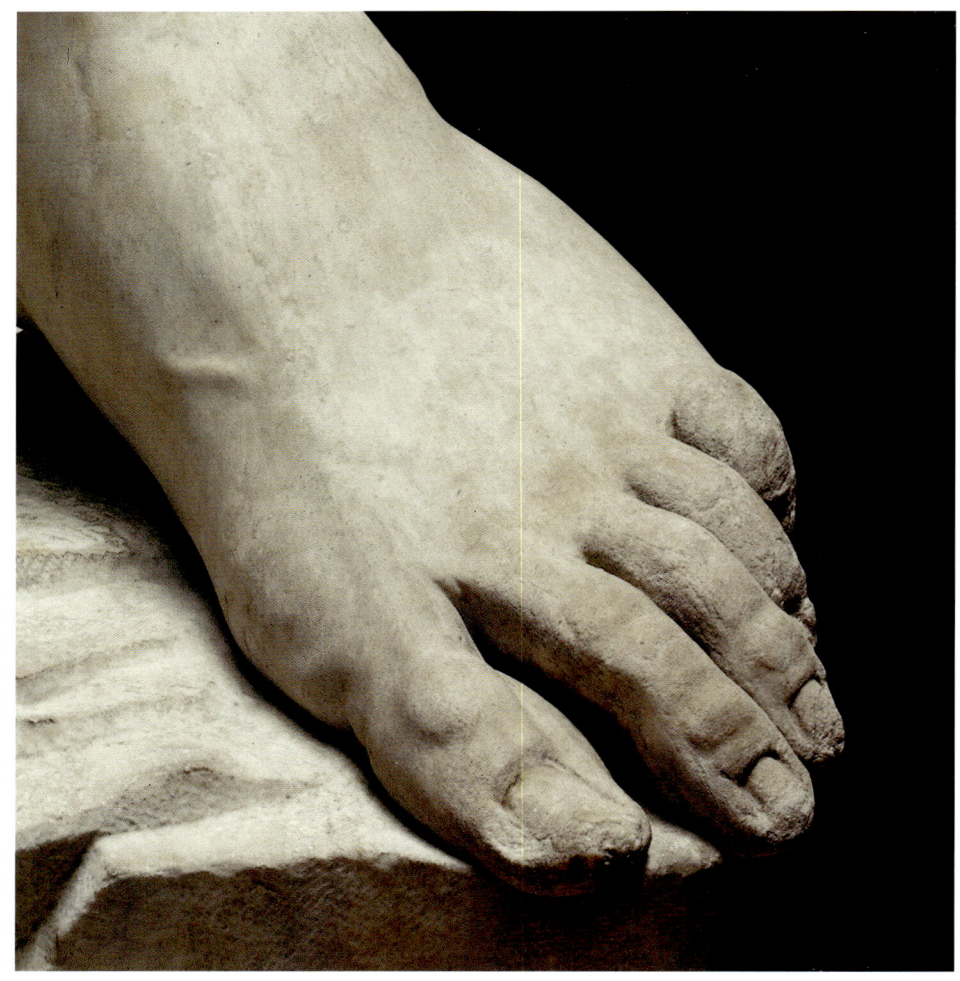
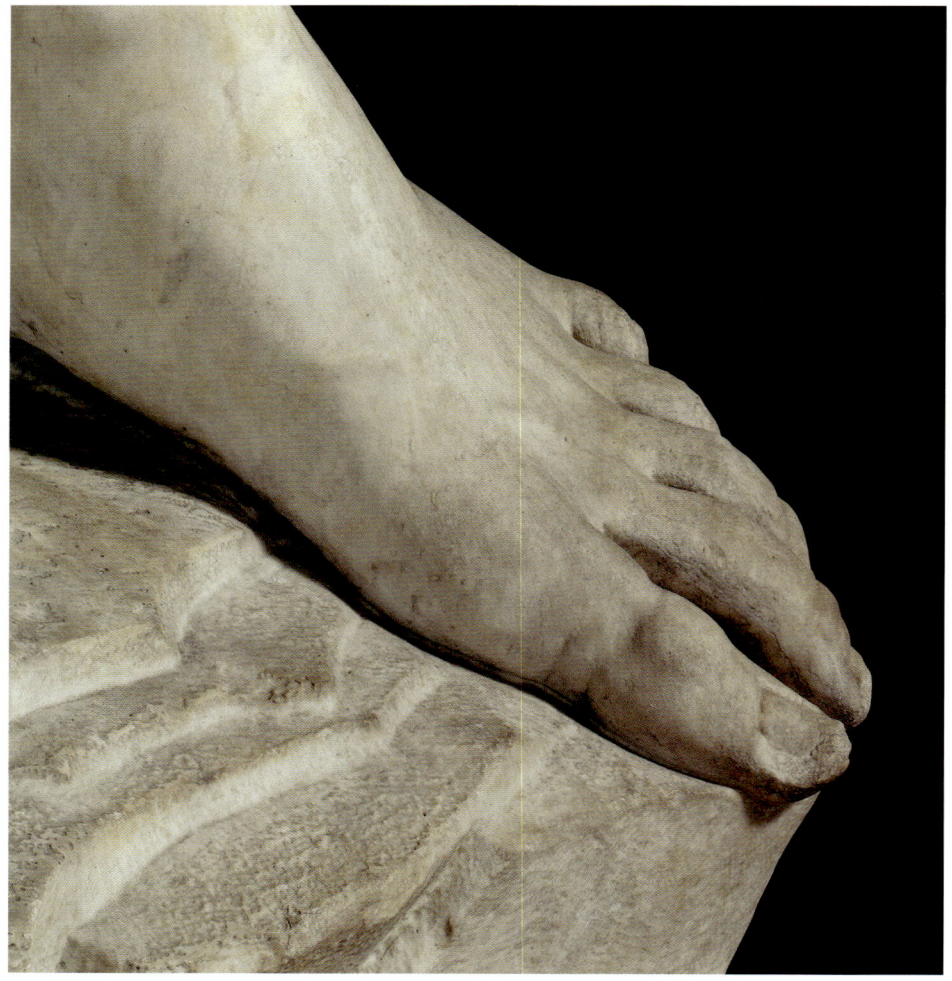

68   A PORTRAIT OF THE DAVID

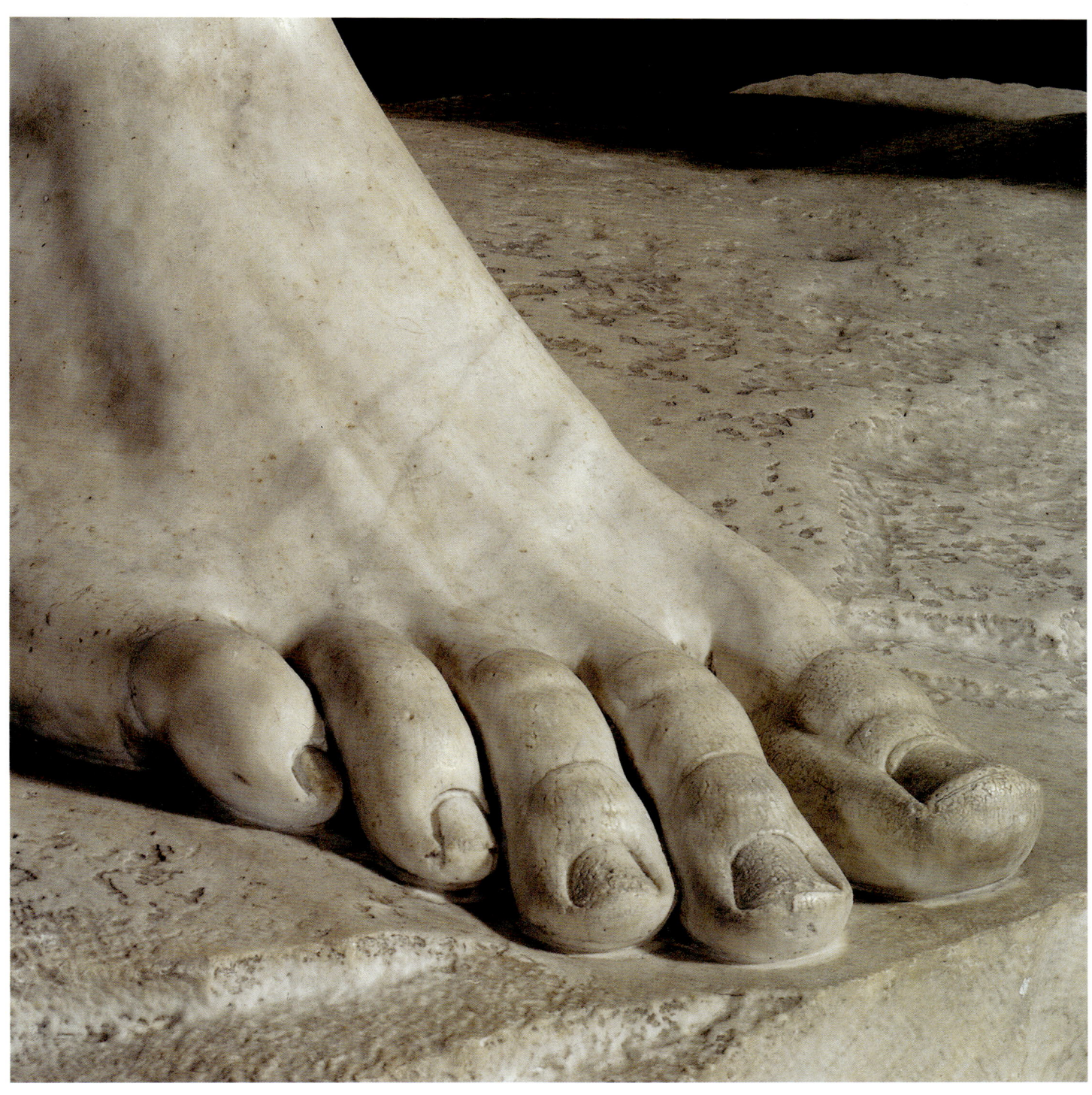

A PORTRAIT OF THE DAVID   69

HISTORY OF A MASTERPIECE

On August 16, 1501, the members of the Opera del Duomo, the Vestry Board of Florence Cathedral, together with the consuls of the Arte della Lana, or Wool Guild, assigned Michelangelo the task of carving a "Giant" from a large block of marble left unused for years in the storerooms of the Opera del Duomo.

Vasari says that the block "was nine *braccia* [arms] high, and unluckily one Simone da Fiesole had begun a giant cutting between the legs and mauling it so badly that the wardens of Santa Maria del Fiore had abandoned it …"

In reality we know from the documents that it was the Florentine sculptor Agostino di Duccio, and not Simone da Fiesole, who had received the commission in 1464 for a gigantic figure of *David*, intended to adorn one of the external buttresses in the apsidal section of the cathedral. To do the work the sculptor had procured in Carrara a single block of marble of colossal dimensions, and not four pieces, as envisaged in the contract, asking and receiving special recompense owing to the difficulty of the undertaking. However, Agostino left the statue unfinished and so, in 1476, the job of completing it was given to Antonio Rossellino, but without any result. Finally, in the June of 1501, the Cathedral Vestry Board decided to look for a sculptor capable of carrying out the work.

At that time the twenty-six-year-old Michelangelo had just returned to Florence from Rome, where he had made a great impression with the *Pietà* now in St. Peter's, and there can be no doubt that he was anxious to show what he was made of in Florence as well.

According to Vasari it was Michelangelo who put himself forward as a candidate for the *David*, as Andrea Sansovino had also done, and the gonfalonier of the Florentine republic, Pier Soderini, played a primary role in the assignment of the work to Buonarroti.

In any case, execution of the work looked like a particularly arduous venture, as it required Michelangelo to fulfill the Humanistic aspiration of carving a colossus of marble to rival the examples of antiquity, a challenge that other artists before him had failed to meet. At the same time Buonarroti had also to tackle the problem of the material, on which someone else's scalpel had already worked and which may also have been of poor quality, filled with flaws. After all, there must have been a good reason why such a large block of marble had been left unused. Its cutting in the quarry of the Fantiscritti, in the Apuan Alps above Carrara, and its transport to Florence first by sea, and then along the course of the Arno, had required an investment of effort and money that could not be allowed to go to waste.

On September 13, 1501, Michelangelo set to work, away from prying eyes inside an enclosure that he built himself in the courtyard of the Opera del Duomo. Vasari tells us that the artist "examined it afresh, and decided that it could be hewn into something new," making a wax model. Unfortunately no model connected with *David* seems to have survived, although there are several drawings documenting the phase of preparation and study preceding the working of the marble: a study for the right arm in the Louvre and another study of an arm in the Uffizi. In addition, a study of a nude in the Louvre based on an ancient statue has been linked with the *David* by Tolnay, the greatest expert on Michelangelo.

An account of a meeting with Michelangelo at a later stage in his life may help us to picture how the artist set about his task. In 1578 the French traveler Blaise de Vigenère wrote: "I saw Michelangelo at work. He had passed his sixtieth year and although he was not very strong, yet in a quarter of an hour he caused more splinters to fall from a very hard block of marble than three young masons in three or four times as long, something almost incredible for those who have not seen it. And I thought that the whole work would be shattered into pieces, as he moved with such force and haste, showering the floor with large splinters, three or four fingers thick, at a single blow. So well aimed was this blow that if he had gone just a tiny bit further than necessary, he would have risked losing everything, since he would not have been able to repair or remodel the work, as is done with images in clay or stucco."

We know that Michelangelo passed directly from the preparatory studies to the block of marble, and that he proceeded by working on successive and parallel layers, first on the principal face, then on the others. This method is perfectly recognizable in such unfinished works as the *Saint Matthew* and the *Prisoners* in the Galleria dell'Accademia in Florence, and there can be no doubt that Michelangelo took the same approach to the *David*. In addition, a close and thorough examination of the sculpture (which has to be considered one of the artist's finished works) reveals marks left by tools that were not usually employed in the finishing stage. Among these is the claw chisel, an instrument with a toothed edge that leaves parallel scores, more or less fine and close together depending on the type used. The marks left by the claw chisel, evident on the forehead, above the eyebrows, form an area of shadow between the eyes and the hair that serves to impart more intensity to the gaze.

Light traces of the claw chisel are visible at other points of the body, creating an effect on the surface of the marble that disrupts the uniformity of the polishing, almost producing an impression of the skin and its natural wrinkles. The hair, on the other hand, bears the marks of the drill, the principal tool employed by Greek and Roman sculptors, which Michelangelo was to stop using in subsequent works.

So Michelangelo worked hard on the statue and two and a half years later it was almost finished. On January 25, 1504, when the sculpture was nearly complete, a commission made up largely of artists was invited, at the request of Michelangelo and the consuls of the Arte della Lana, to express its views on the best place to locate it. Among the members of the commission were painters like the elderly Sandro Botticelli, Leonardo da Vinci, Filippino Lippi, Piero di Cosimo, Francesco Granacci, Cosimo Rosselli and Lorenzo di Credi and sculptors and architects like Andrea della Robbia, Andrea Sansovino, Cronaca, Francesco Monciatto, Giuliano and Antonio da Sangallo. It is not known exactly why the possibility of locating the work on the outside of the cathedral had been discarded. We do know, however, that the meeting of the commission was opened by Maestro Francesco, herald of the Signoria, who put forward two solutions, declaring his preference for the first: in front of the entrance of the Palazzo della Signoria, in the place of Donatello's *Judith*, or in the courtyard of the same building, on the spot where Verrocchio's bronze *David* stood. The members of the commission advanced various proposals and the fierce debate that preceded the final decision laid bare tensions and animosity between the artists, as well as bringing out the political implications of what was apparently an artistic choice. Some continued to suggest a location on the outside of the cathedral, as had originally been planned. Among these, the carpenter Francesco Monciatto declared that he did not understand why the statue should no longer be placed on one of the buttresses of the cathedral, while Botticelli and Cosimo Rosselli advised erecting the *David* on a tall pedestal in front of the church. Its placement in the Loggia della Signoria, recommended by the sculptor and architect Giuliano da Sangallo, became the most plausible alternative to the location in front of the palace. This idea, which was supported by Leonardo among others, took into account the problems of conservation of the sculpture, carved from a block of "soft" marble that had already been exposed to water for a long time. Other artists suggested leaving the choice to its creator, as no one was better suited than he to deciding where the statue should be erected. In the end what prevailed was the most prestigious location, in front of the Palazzo della Signoria. It was probably the one preferred by Michelangelo who, while not present at the meeting, was unlikely to have played no part in the final decision.

In May 1504 the sculpture was at last transported to Piazza della Signoria. The event is recorded not only by Vasari, but also by several chroniclers of the day, who stressed both the difficulty of the undertaking and the tense atmosphere in the city at the time it was carried out. The "strong wooden frame" from which Vasari said the *David* was suspended with ropes for the journey from the Opera del Duomo to the square was designed and built under the guidance of Cronaca, with the collaboration of numerous Florentine craftsmen and architects, including Antonio da Sangallo, Baccio d'Agnolo and Bernardo della Cecca. In his *Diario fiorentino dal 1450 al 1516*, the chronicler Luca Landucci recounts: "And on May 14, 1504 the marble giant was taken from the Opera. It came out at midnight and they broke down the wall above the door so that it could pass through, and that night the Giant was pelted with stones in an attempt to damage it. It had to be guarded at night, and went very slowly and was bound upright, so that it hung without touching the ground with its feet, with strong beams and great ingenuity, and took four days to reach the piazza: it arrived there on May 18 at twelve o'clock, and four greased timbers were placed under it, and which were changed from time to time, and it took until June 8, 1504, to hoist it onto the balustrade, where stood the *Judith*, which had to be removed."

After the transfer of the *David* onto the "balustrade" of the Palazzo della Signoria (i.e. the balcony from which crowds were addressed), in the place of Donatello's *Judith and Holofernes*, Cronaca and Antonio da Sangallo were given the task of creating a pedestal for the sculpture, while Michelangelo spent another four months giving the statue its finishing touches, in the yard set up around it. There is no record of the technique and materials used by Michelangelo for this operation, but it is legitimate to assume that the artist gave it some kind of protective coating. Unfortunately the statue's long exposure to the weather and the restorations it underwent in the 19th century have removed all trace of such substances.

On September 8, 1504, the feast day of the Virgin Mary, the *David* was unveiled to the public. A partial gilding set off the strap of the sling and the "prop," i.e. the trunk placed behind the hero's right leg, and the garland made of brass wire with twenty-eight copper leaves, probably placed on his head, was also gilded.

A few days prior to the unveiling of the sculpture, Michelangelo received the balance of the agreed payment: four hundred scudi, a considerable but not exceptional sum if we bear in mind the scale of the work and the length of time it took.

David was immediately recognized as a masterpiece and nicknamed the Giant by the Florentines, who thus assigned him the same epithet usually given to his adversary Goliath. The work marked an epoch and established Michelangelo's reputation as the sculptor who had surpassed the ancients.

David is a young and completely naked man, the first large statue of a nude since Roman times, and his posture, with one leg bearing his weight and the other left free, recalls the attitude of the heroes of classical times. The nudity of the figure testifies to the artist's extraordinary knowledge of human anatomy and, at the same time, takes on a symbolic significance. David naked and unarmed before Goliath is invincible because he is protected by God. Michelangelo has renewed the iconography of the Biblical personage: he is not telling his story, but creating the ideal figure of a hero. So Goliath's head does not lie at his feet, as in the traditional iconography, and David seems to be represented some time prior to the combat, but not at a precise moment.

Set in front of the seat of power, the *David* was straightaway regarded as the political and moral symbol of the city of Florence, and was defined by Vasari as the "emblem of the Palace."

Its physical proximity to the seat of the city's government meant that the sculpture was caught up in the events that left a mark on the history of Florence in the 16th century. In 1512, when Pier Soderini was exiled and the rule of the Medici family restored, a bolt of lightning damaged the base of the statue, with grave consequences for the stability of the work. In the 19th century this was used as an argument in support of the removal of the colossus from Piazza della Signoria. Subsequently, in 1527, during the riots that accompanied the expulsion of the Medici and the short-lived reinstatement of the republic, the statue's left arm was broken into pieces: this was the most serious harm done to the *David* in the past. In his *Life* of Francesco Salviati Vasari relates that it was a bench, thrown from a window of Palazzo Vecchio, which damaged the sculpture. The pieces of the arm, left unnoticed on the ground, were picked up by Salviati and Vasari himself, both very young at the time, and taken to Salviati's father. The latter, after keeping the fragments for several years, handed them over to Duke Cosimo I, who had them reattached to the statue with copper pins in 1543. This was the first act of restoration to which the work was subjected. Nineteenth-century literature records further damage inflicted on the *David* at an unspecified time, when the breakage of a gutter on Palazzo Vecchio washed away part of the surface. Today, however, it is impossible to distinguish the harm caused by the breaking of the gutter from that due to the statue's long exposure to the weather.

In the 19th century the problem of the conservation of the *David* became one of the crucial topics of discussion in the city. The restoration carried out by Corrado Ricci dates from 1813: it was the first modern and documented intervention in Michelangelo's masterpiece. The restorer, charged with replacing the middle finger of the right hand that had been broken in unknown circumstances, cleaned the statue as well and deemed it necessary to cover the entire surface with encaustic, a protective layer of wax applied while hot. Traces of this procedure, which reflected the neoclassical taste for shiny and polished marble, could still be detected prior to the last, most recent restoration. However, this intervention had serious repercussions on the preservation of the statue as it was later subjected to extremely heavy-handed scrubbings, with the precise aim of removing the wax of the encaustic.

The most drastic intervention was that carried out in 1843 by Aristodemo Costoli, who used a fifty-percent solution of hydrochloric acid and sharp-edged tools to remove the hardest layers of crust on the statue. The restoration had the full support of the sculptor Lorenzo Bartolini, then adviser to the board in charge of royal construction works, although he also showed a great interest in the problem of the *David's* conservation and had been the first, in 1842, to propose shifting the statue out of the square and placing it under cover. As a result of the alarm raised by Bartolini Grand Duke Leopold II commissioned a plaster cast of the *David* from the sculptor Clemente Papi, to be used to make a bronze copy with which to replace the original in Piazza della Signoria. This rather irresponsible initiative, carried out on a work that was displaying problems of stability, was not without consequences for the conservation of the sculpture. At the same time the realization of the plaster copy was providential, as all subsequent total and partial casts of the *David* have been made from Papi's, preserved in the collection of plaster casts of the Istituto Statale d'Arte in Florence.

From 1852 onward the proposal to move the *David* began to gain ground, but it proved hard to reach agreement on a new location for the masterpiece. Among those put forward, the Loggia della Signoria seems to have enjoyed a fair amount of support, but when it was tried out, with the temporary erection of the plaster cast under the loggia, reactions were negative and the proposal was rejected.

Between 1860 and 1870 the debate over the *David's* fate began to tilt in the direction of a definitive solution in which Michelangelo's sculpture would be removed from Piazza della Signoria. In 1872 the *David* was enclosed in a wooden framework and hidden from view. The decision to move the work had now been taken and in the summer of 1873 the statue was taken to the Accademia di Belle Arti. The transport of the sculpture, slung from a wooden structure whose model is conserved in the museum of Casa Buonarroti, was done on rails and took ten days, from July 30 to August 8. The original pedestal, made to a design by Antonio da Sangallo and Cronaca, was destroyed. At the Accademia the *David* remained crated up until 1882, while the tribune designed to house the statue was built around it. The project was entrusted to Emilio De Fabris, considered the most authoritative architect in Florence, following his victory in the competition for the new façade of the cathedral of Santa Maria del Fiore. The result is one of the most significant examples of the 19th-century mode of celebrating a work of art: the *David* was located at the center of an exedra with an apse like that of a church. Constructed with a modern system of skylights that illuminate the statue from above, the tribune is preceded by a sort of nave that determines the route of approach to Michelangelo's masterpiece. Since 1909, on the initiative of Corrado Ricci, head of the Fine Arts Service at the time, this route has been lined with four of the unfinished *Prisoners* originally carved for the tomb of Julius II, brought from the Grotta del Buontalenti in the Boboli Gardens, and the statue of *Saint Matthew*, also incomplete, intended for the cathedral. In 1940 they were joined by the *Palestrina Pietà*, after its acquisition by the Italian State.

The location in the tribune brings out the gigantic dimensions of every detail and allows observers to walk all the way round the statue. Intended to be seen from all sides and no longer, as in medieval statuary, just from the front, the *David* in fact has four privileged points of view: front, right side, rear and left side, corresponding to the route followed around the work by hundreds of visitors every day. The frontal point of view remains indisputably the principal one. It allows us to admire the beauty of the forms, to notice the slight internal imbalances, such as the oversized right hand, and to perceive the energy of the figure, which is concentrated in the twisting of the head and the tense expression on the face. We know, however, that the perspective effect of seeing the sculpture inside the tribune is different from what it would have been in Piazza della Signoria. In fact, by choice of the architect De Fabris, the height of the pedestal constructed for the statue in the Galleria dell'Accademia corresponds to the viewpoint of the old "balcony" of Palazzo Vecchio and not that of someone in the square.

After the transfer of the *David* to the Accademia the square remained for a long time without one of its most significant features. The attempt to fill the void with the bronze copy made in 1866 was rejected by the Florentines, who were not willing to accept a *David* that differed in material and color from the original one. So the bronze copy was erected at the center of the panoramic square named after Michelangelo and laid out by Giuseppe Poggi on the ring roads, together with copies, also in bronze, of the allegorical figures from the Medici tombs in the New Sacristy of San Lorenzo. Finally, in 1910, Luigi Arrighetti's marble copy of the *David* was set up in Piazza della Signoria.

THE RESTORATION OF THE STATUE

In September 1991 the *David* suffered an act of vandalism in which the second toe of the left foot was broken in several places. Following this unfortunate episode a monitoring system was set up to keep a constant watch on the statue's state of preservation. This was followed, in the spring of 2002, by the development of a complete program of scientific investigations to be carried out internally and externally, as well as into the environment in which the work is housed. The research conducted on some fragments recovered after the attack was supplemented by other internal examinations of the sculpture (gamma-ray photographs, i.e. images made under gamma radiation that are capable of penetrating the marble, and thermographs), which have made it possible to locate the pins inserted in the arm that was fractured in 1527. But it was the visual observations, some of them carried out with the aid of the microscope, and the tests performed on the statue that provided the specific data of most use in suggesting how to proceed with the work of restoration.

Finally, on-going studies of the climate and air pollution in the immediate surroundings of the statue are aimed at determining whether and to what extent the large number of visitors has an effect on its state of preservation.

The analysis of this enormous amount of information has revealed some highly interesting facts, in the first place the exact measurements of the *David*, which is 17 feet high (516 centimeters), weighs 6.2 tons (5,660 kilograms) and has a surface area of 210 square feet (19.47 square meters). The results of the diagnostic investigations and visual observations have also brought to light three different types of defect, the original flaws in the marble, the deposits on its surface and the breaks; they have also made it possible to identify traces of Michelangelo's work.

The significant quantity of veining and of small cavities, the so-called *taròli*, is due to the nature of the material itself, while the substantial wear found on the upper part of the head and the shoulders can be traced to the action of rainwater, which has affected the most exposed areas and dates from the

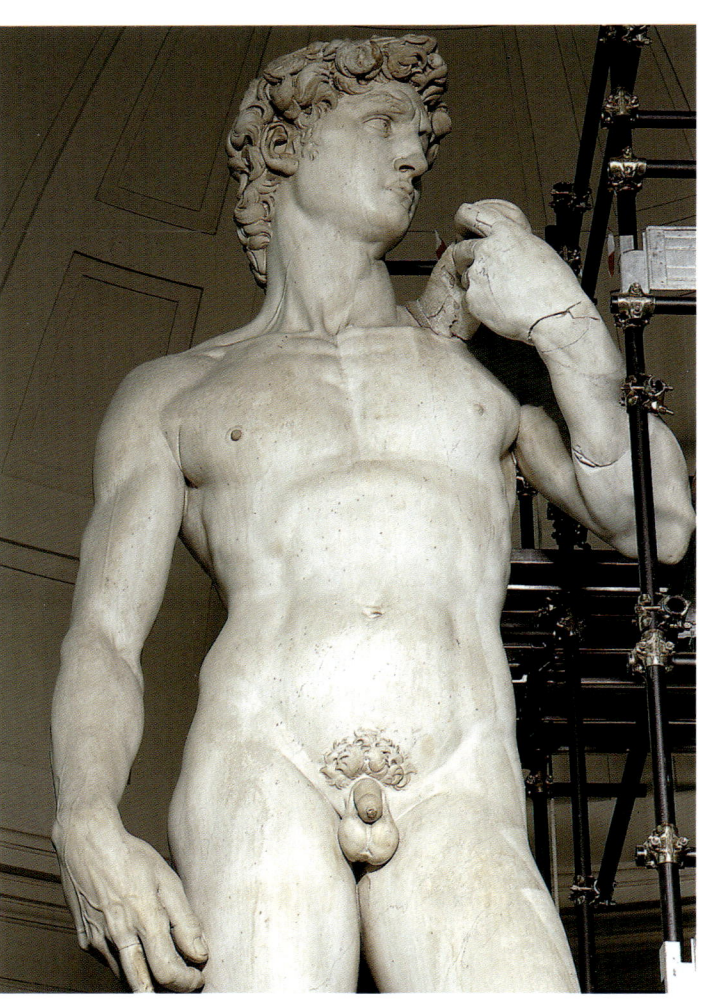

period in which the statue was located in the open. The modeling of the marble also appears to have been conditioned at several points, especially on the upper part of the back, as a result of the way in which the block had been worked by Agostino di Duccio in 1464 and Antonio Rossellino in 1476. In addition to the scratches visible in various places, the most obvious fracture is that of the left arm and hand, broken off during the Florentine riots of April 26, 1527.

However, the greatest contribution to the deterioration in the *David's* state comes from the drastic restoration carried out by Aristodemo Costoli in 1843, in which overly aggressive solvents were used, triggering a process of corrosion of the sculpture's surface. Moreover, all trace of any original protective treatment was removed in the course of the numerous restorations carried out in previous centuries and there is currently no hope of ever being able to find it again.

The surface of the *David* also showed residual traces of plaster from the cast made by Clemente Papi in 1847, a number of so-called "black encrustations" (sulfate residues of air pollution), numerous spots of wax, perhaps from the torches used to illuminate Piazza della Signoria, and purple stains caused by organic residues of microorganisms that had grown on the surface of the marble in the past. Finally, *David's* ankles and the trunk against which his right leg rests are traversed by numerous horizontal cracks, already detected in the 19th century, whose principal cause has been identified as subsidence of the foundation.

All these data convinced the scientific commission whose job it was to evaluate the *David's* state of preservation of the need for a new intervention: the work began on September 16, 2002, and was concluded on May 24, 2004.

The first phase consisted of fact-finding investigations that allowed a precise mapping of the sculpture's conditions of preservation. This was followed by a delicate cleaning that served to remove deposits of dust, the numerous drippings of wax and the minimal traces of sulfation identified by the analyses. To eliminate each of these foreign substances, trial cleanings were carried out at several points on the surface of the sculpture, differing in their state of preservation or type of working.

In addition to the cleaning, the interven-

tion entailed removal of the putty used to fill the fracture lines in the left arm and its replacement with more suitable material, a mixture of lime and powdered marble of various colors, so as to obtain a result closer to the tonality of the original marble. Finally, the most obvious holes in the marble, the aforementioned *taròli* or pores, which can compromise the work's state of preservation by forming traps for dust and pollutants of various origins, have been filled.

The results achieved by the restoration relate primarily to the aesthetics of the work, but are also significant with regard to the sculpture's stability and preservation. In fact while the *David* now has a more balanced appearance in terms of the relations of light and shade, as well as presenting a cleaner definition of the modeling, the replacement of the putty in the fractures of the left arm ensures the necessary stability at a point that is particularly fragile and exposed, and the removal of the residues of plaster and the filling of the *taròli* guarantees better protection and easier maintenance.

THE LIFE OF MICHELANGELO

"Thus in 1474 the true and noble wife of Ludovico di Lionardo Buonarroti Simone, said to be of the ancient and noble family of the Counts of Canossa, gave birth to a son in the Casentino, under a lucky star."

These are the words with which Giorgio Vasari, the multifaceted painter, architect and writer from Arezzo famous for his biographies of the principal Italian artists of the 14th, 15th and 16th centuries, chose to open his celebrated account of Michelangelo's life. The bombastic tone reflects the author's belief that he was describing an exceptional existence and personality. In fact we know that Vasari had conceived his literary work as a celebration of Buonarroti, whom he regarded as the culmination and apotheosis of the entire history of art: Michelangelo embodied the ideal of the Renaissance artist who was able to tackle every discipline with success and to develop his own theory of art.

So Michelangelo Buonarroti was born on March 6, 1475, at Caprese, a small town not far from Arezzo where his father Lodovico held the post of podestà (magistrate). The same year, Lodovico's term of office at an end, the family returned to their city of origin, Florence, where the young Michelangelo spent his childhood and began his training as an artist. Going against the wishes of his father, who had enrolled him in a school of grammar at the age of six, with an eye to a future career in politics, the young Michelangelo soon declared his intention to devote himself to art, displaying extraordinary gifts.

In 1488 a contract was drawn up with Domenico Ghirlandaio, one of the most renowned artists in Florence at the time and head of a flourishing workshop in which Michelangelo was to have served three years of apprenticeship. But his stay in Ghirlandaio's workshop was much shorter than planned: in fact he left the following year, 1489, as a result of disagreements with the master. During his apprenticeship Michelangelo witnessed and may even have contributed to Ghirlandaio's decoration of the Tornabuoni Chapel in Santa Maria Novella. According to the sources, the artist painted one of his earliest works in this period: now lost, it was a panel copy of

Facing page,
Giuliano
Bugiardini
(attributed),
*Portrait of
Michelangelo in
a Turban.*
Casa Buonarroti,
Florence

Emilio Zocchi,
*Michelangelo as
a Boy.*
Galleria Palatina,
Florence

Saint Anthony Beaten by Devils, an engraving from the 15th-century cycle of the *Temptations of Saint Anthony* by Martin Schongauer.

Michelangelo, *Madonna of the Stairs*. Casa Buonarroti, Florence

Michelangelo, *Crucifix*. Sacristy of Santo Spirito, Florence

Around 1489 Michelangelo was introduced to the garden of San Marco, a place owned by the Medici family where an interesting experiment had been under way for several years: part of the family's collection of ancient sculptures, probably accompanied by drawings and models by modern sculptors, was placed at the disposal of young artists so that they could study them under the guidance of Bertoldo di Giovanni. This can be seen as the first attempt to set up an academy for the instruction of young artists, and sculptors in particular, offering them an alternative to the period of technical training in a workshop. In the garden of San Marco Michelangelo caught the attention of Lorenzo the Magnificent, who even lodged him in his palace on Via Larga (now via Cavour) for about two years. This brought him into contact with the learned men in Lorenzo's circle, including the poet and scholar Politian, and allowed him to study the valuable Medici collection of carved gems and applied art.

Michelangelo's interest in antiquity, together with his study of the great artists of the more recent past such as Masaccio and, somewhat earlier, Giotto, is documented by several drawings, but above all it is reflected in his first works of sculpture, the *Madonna of the Stairs* (Casa Buonarroti, Florence) executed in 1490 and the unfinished marble bas-relief representing the *Battle of the Centaurs* (Casa Buonarroti, Florence), probably begun in 1491.

To understand Michelangelo's artistic language fully we must also bear in mind his studies of anatomy, made possible by the prior of the Augustinian monastery of Santo Spirito, who allowed Michelangelo to use a room in the complex to carry out the dissection of cadavers. In these same years, between 1492 and 1494, Buonarroti carved a wooden *Crucifix* (sacristy of Santo Spirito, Florence) for the same monastery: its attribution is still disputed by some scholars but the refined articulation of the members, founded on a thorough investigation of anatomy, means that it fits well into the course of Michelangelo's artistic development.

Michelangelo, *Battle of the Centaurs*. Casa Buonarroti, Florence

In 1494, following the death of Lorenzo de' Medici and the ensuing changes in the Florentine political situation, Michelangelo left the city, first for Venice and then Bologna. Here the artist stayed for over a year as he was assigned the prestigious task of completing the *Tomb of Saint Dominic*, the monumental marble shrine and sepulcher in the church of San Domenico for which Buonarroti executed the three missing sculptures of *Saint Petronius*, *Saint Proculus* and an *Angel Holding a Candlestick*. The highly expressive characterization of the figures makes them stand out from the rest of the tomb, realized at different times by Nicola Pisano and Niccolò dell'Arca.

Toward the end of 1495 or at the beginning of the following year, the artist returned to Florence, where he again established ties with the Medici family, carving for Lorenzo the Magnificent's cousin Lorenzo di Pierfrancesco a sculpture of the *Infant Saint John* of which no trace remains. In this period Michelangelo also sculpted a small *Sleeping Cupid*, now lost, which was purchased by Cardinal Raffaele Riario in Rome as an antique. The skill he had displayed in this "forgery" prompted Cardinal Riario to summon Michelangelo to work for him in Rome. So on June 25, 1496, the artist left Florence for the Eternal City.

THE LIFE OF MICHELANGELO   83

The first work that Michelangelo executed in the summer of that same year was a statue of *Bacchus* (Museo Nazionale del Bargello, Florence), in which the god of wine is represented in an obviously drunken state and a highly unstable pose. The sculpture would later be acquired by the Roman banker Jacopo Galli, who owned another of the master's works, an *Apollo* or *Cupid* that has recently been tentatively identified with the *Young Archer* (Services Culturels de l'Ambassade de France, New York).

In 1496 the artist executed a cartoon, now lost, of *Saint Francis Receiving the Stigmata* for a relative of Cardinal Riario, while in the summer of 1497 there is a record of his purchasing a panel of wood. Many scholars believe the panel in question to have been the one on which he painted the *Manchester Madonna* (National Gallery, London), named after the city in which it was exhibited for the first time in 1857. The critics are still divided on this attribution: while many are ready to assign the work to Michelangelo's youth, others allocate it, along with another small group of paintings, to an anonymous artist given the conventional name of the "Master of the Manchester Madonna." Another painting ascribed to Michelangelo, although with greater caution, that displays many parallels with the *Manchester Madonna* is the *Entombment of Christ* (National Gallery, London). Both works are in an unfinished state, are characterized by a very high quality of execution and face the same doubts over their attribution.

In 1499 Michelangelo sculpted the most significant masterpiece of his youth, the *Pietà* (St. Peter's, Rome), executed for the French Cardinal Jean Bilhères de Lagraulas, ambassador of King Charles VIII to the pontiff. Although he was still only twenty-four, Michelangelo had by now developed his personal artistic language to the full: the Vatican *Pietà* is a highly poetic composition, in which technical ability and formal composure are harmoniously fused in perfect equilibrium.

In republican Florence two years later, Michelangelo obtained an impressive series of prestigious commissions: from that of the altar in Siena Cathedral, for which he carved four of the fifteen figures ordered from him on June 5, 1501 by Cardinal Francesco Todeschini Piccolomini, to the one he received on April 24, 1502, for twelve statues of apostles for Florence Cathedral. He never got further than the *Saint Matthew* (Galleria dell'Accademia, Florence), executed about two years later, and even that was never finished. On August

Michelangelo, *Saint Matthew*. Galleria dell'Accademia, Florence

Facing page, Michelangelo, *Pitti Tondo*, detail. Museo Nazionale del Bargello, Florence

16, 1501, he signed a contract with the Vestry Board of Florence Cathedral and in exchange was given a block of Carrara marble, already rough-hewn by other sculptors. From this marble was born the *David*, the statue that, in Vasari's words, "bears the palm among all modern and ancient works" and which firmly established the artist's reputation.

In addition, Michelangelo carved two marble tondi (circular reliefs) for members of two distinguished Florentine families: the *Taddei Tondo* (Royal Academy of Arts, London) and the *Pitti Tondo* (Museo Nazionale del Bargello, Florence). Both were executed around 1503 and left incomplete in 1505, at the time of Michelangelo's departure for Rome. The circular format was also adopted by the artist in the large picture commissioned by Agnolo Doni and painted before the end of the first decade of the century: the *Doni Tondo* (Galleria degli Uffizi, Florence) was described by Vasari as "the most finished and beautiful" of Michelangelo's paintings and won the unreserved admiration of his contemporaries.

In 1504 the Gonfalonier of Justice of the Florentine republic, Pier Soderini, entrusted Buonarroti with the execution of a large fresco in

Michelangelo, *Doni Tondo*. Galleria degli Uffizi, Florence

Michelangelo, *Bruges Madonna*. Notre Dame, Bruges

Michelangelo, *Project for the Tomb of Julius II.* Gabinetto dei Disegni e delle Stampe degli Uffizi, Florence

A view of the Sistine Chapel

the Sala del Gran Consiglio of the Palazzo della Signoria. The decoration of the room had already seen Leonardo engaged, since April 1503, in the representation of the *Battle of Anghiari*; Michelangelo was to depict the *Battle of Cascina* against the Pisans, a clash that ended in the victory of the Florentines in 1364. Thanks to the copy of Michelangelo's cartoon made around 1542 by Aristotile da Sangallo (Leicester Collection, Holkham Hall, Norfolk), we can still appreciate the complex composition conceived by Buonarroti but never actually painted on the walls of the palace.

The *Bruges Madonna* (Notre Dame, Bruges), sculpted for the Mouscron family, originally from Flanders, and another *David* cast in bronze for Marshal Pierre de Rohan but now lost, were the last works executed by Michelangelo at the time of the republic of Florence. In fact the artist was summoned by Pope Julius II della Rovere, who entrusted him with the task of sculpting his tomb in St. Peter's.

So around 1505 Michelangelo left Florence for Rome, where he was to embark on a new and difficult adventure. The "tragedy of the tomb," as he himself would define the tormented history of the realization of the pope's sepulchral monument, was to last with changing fortunes for several decades, punctuated by fierce quarrels between the two proud and intractable protagonists, followed by reconciliations. The commission would not be completed until 1547, with the erection of the monument in the church of San Pietro in Vincoli, in a form much reduced from its original conception. For the tomb Michelangelo carved the *Prisoners* (Musée du Louvre, Paris, and Galleria dell'Accademia, Florence), the imposing and vigorous *Moses* and figures of Leah and Rachel, symbolizing the active and contemplative life. *Moses* and the female figures are the only statues that are still part of Julius II's monument.

In the November of 1506 Michelangelo was in Bologna to execute a bronze portrait-bust of Julius II; the sculpture, formally mounted on the façade of the church of San Petronio in Feb-

THE LIFE OF MICHELANGELO

ruary 1508, would remain there for only three years, before being destroyed in 1511.

In May 1508 Julius II asked the artist to renew the pictorial decoration of the ceiling of the Sistine Chapel, in which deep cracks had appeared several years earlier. The cycle of frescoes that Michelangelo painted is striking in its dimensions and the number of figures represented, but also and above all in the complexity of the iconographic program, in which ideas drawn from neoplatonic teachings are effectively combined with scenes from the Bible. The refined symphony of colors orchestrated by Michelangelo, brought back to their original splendor by the restoration of the frescoes carried out between 1980 and 1989, contributes to the stunning effect of the ceiling of the Sistine Chapel, which was officially inaugurated by Julius II on November 1, 1512.

On the death of Julius II in 1513, the new pontiff, Leo X de' Medici, involved the artist in his project for the "rebirth" of Florence, entrusting him with a series of interventions in the basilica of San Lorenzo, under Medici patronage. These ranged from the completion of the façade to the design and sculptural decoration of a mortuary chapel, the New Sacristy, destined to house the remains of several members of the family.

The undertaking, which grew even more ambitious with the construction of the Biblioteca Laurenziana at the behest of another Medici pope, Clement VII, in 1524, dragged on for years. Indeed, it would never be finished as Michelangelo went back to Rome in 1534, to complete the decoration of the Sistine Chapel with the execution of the *Last Judgment*. During these years in Florence the artist also carved a *Risen Christ* in marble for Metello Vari; the work, once finished, was transported to Rome by a trusted assistant and set up in the church of Santa Maria sopra Minerva.

Over the brief lifetime of the second Florentine republic, reestablished following the Sack of Rome in 1527, Michelangelo was appointed "commissioner general for all the fortifications" and in this role made

Michelangelo, Staircase of the Biblioteca Laurenziana. Florence

Michelangelo, *Moses*. San Pietro in Vincoli, Rome

Facing page, Michelangelo, *The Dying Slave*, detail. Musée du Louvre, Paris

many journeys to various cities of the peninsula to study different types of defense. During his stay in Ferrara in July 1529, Michelangelo met Duke Alfonso I d'Este, ruler of the city and his great admirer, who asked him to execute a work for him. Back in Florence, he painted a *Leda*, finished in 1530 and lost over the course of time but fortunately known to us through copies made by other artists.

At almost the same time Michelangelo drew a cartoon for a *Noli me tangere*, requested from him by Alfonso d'Avalos who wanted to present it to his aunt, Vittoria Colonna, the poet who was to develop a close friendship with Buonarroti in later years. The cartoon, probably completed in 1531, was turned into a painting by Pontormo, working under the master's supervision and finishing the picture between the end of 1531 and the beginning of 1532. Sometime around 1533 Pontormo executed another picture to a preparatory cartoon by Michelangelo, the painting of *Venus and Cupid* for the Florentine merchant and banker Bartolomeo Bettini (Galleria dell'Accademia, Florence). In his final years in Florence Michelangelo also sculpted an *Apollo-David* in marble (Museo del Bargello, Florence) and the *Victory* (Palazzo Vecchio, Florence).

In 1534, the year of Pope Clement VII's death, Michelangelo went back to Rome for good, closing his relations with Florence forever. Under the pontificate of Paul III Michelangelo returned to the Sistine Chapel about twenty-four years after concluding the frescoes on the ceiling, to paint the splendid *Last Judgment*. The year 1536 marked the beginning of a task that was to occupy the sixty-year-old Michelangelo for around five years, until the official unveiling of the painting on October 31, 1541.

A year later Paul III commissioned him to decorate the rooms of the Pauline Chapel in the Vatican, erected at the behest of the same pope. In 1546 Michelangelo was placed in charge of the construction of St. Peter's. The western part of the basilica was realized under his direction, but it was in the design of the majestic dome, finished after his death, that the artist left his most significant mark on the entire complex of the Vatican. Other architectural works carried out by Michelangelo in these years were the layout of the Piazza del Campidoglio and the church of San Giovanni dei Fiorentini, while the marble bust of *Brutus* (Museo Nazionale del Bargello, Florence) dates from the end of the decade.

Facing page, Michelangelo, *Tomb of Giuliano de' Medici*. Medici Chapels, Florence

Michelangelo, *Victory*. Palazzo Vecchio, Florence

In the meantime Michelangelo's private life was marked by a sad event: his friend Vittoria Colonna died in 1547. The intense relationship between them, grounded in the quest for a new religious spirituality, is fundamental to an understanding of Buonarroti's late sculptures and drawings. Among the drawings he executed for Vittoria Colonna, in fact, are a *Christ Crucified* (British Museum, London) and a *Pietà* (Isabella Stewart Gardner Museum, Boston), both of them identified through descriptions in their correspondence. The sense of religious disquiet that pervades these works is also to be found in his last works of sculpture: a prime example is the *Bandini Pietà* (Museo dell'Opera del Duomo, Florence), carved by Buonarroti around 1553 and perhaps intended for his own tomb. The same meditation on the theme of the deposition underlies the *Palestrina Pietà* (Galleria dell'Accademia, Florence), in which the artist intensified even more the anatomical definition of the figure of Christ. This series of works linked by similar schemes of composition concludes with the *Rondanini Pietà* (Museo del Castello Sforzesco, Milan), on which Michelangelo probably worked right up to the last days of his life. In the final years, between 1560 and 1564, Michelangelo designed the city gate of Porta Pia for Pius IV and worked on the project for the Sforza Chapel in Santa Maria Maggiore.

Michelangelo died in Rome, at the age of eighty-nine, on February 18, 1564, surrounded by his closest friends. The artist's body was temporarily laid to rest in the church of the Santi Apostoli, pending the realization of the tomb that the pope intended to dedicate to him in the basilica of St. Peter. But on the point of death the artist had expressed his desire to be buried in Florence, and so his nephew Leonardo Buonarroti decided to carry off his remains and take them secretly to the Tuscan city.

The solemn funeral of the artist was held in the church of San Lorenzo on July 14, celebrated with great pomp by the members of the Academy. It was attended by the principal political authorities and artistic figures of the time as well as an immense crowd of ordinary people. After the funeral Buonarroti's body was placed, on the orders of Cosimo I de' Medici, in "an honored place in Santa Croce." The monument that contains Michelangelo's remains is the last tribute that Giorgio Vasari paid to his memory, a wall tomb crowned by a mural painting of the *Pietà* and adorned with three marble statues representing *Painting, Sculpture* and *Architecture* mourning the loss of their most inspired interpreter.

Giorgio Vasari, *Tomb of Michelangelo*. Santa Croce, Florence

Facing page, Michelangelo, *Pietà*. Museo dell'Opera del Duomo, Florence

BIBLIOGRAPHY

G. VASARI, *Le vite de' più eccellenti architetti, pittori et scultori italiani, da Cimabue insino a' tempi nostri*, Florence 1550 (second edition Florence 1568; annotated edition by G. Milanesi, Florence 1906). English translations by G.C. de Vere, *Lives of the Painters, Sculptors and Architects*, London 1996 (1912), 2 vols.; G. Bull, *Lives of the Artists* (Volume I), Harmondsworth, 1987 (1965).

A. CONDIVI, *Vita di Michelangelo Buonarroti*, Rome 1553 (ed. by G. Nencioni, Florence 1998). English translation by A.S. Wohl, *The Life of Michelangelo*, University Park (PA) 1999.

E. STEINMANN and R. WITTKOWER, *Michelangelo – Bibliographie 1510-1926*, Leipzig 1927.

C. DE TOLNAY, *Michelangelo Buonarroti*, Princeton 1943-60 (reprint 1969-71).

R.J. CLEMENTS, *Michelangelo's Theory of Art*, New York 1961.

G. VASARI, *La vita di Michelangelo nelle redazioni del 1550 e del 1568*, edited and annotated by P. Barocchi, Milan-Naples 1962.

H. VON EINEM, *Michelangelo*, Berlin 1973.

F. VERSPOHL, "Il David in Piazza della Signoria a Firenze. Michelangelo e Machiavelli," in *Comunità*, 37, 1983, pp. 291-356.

J. ELKINS, "Michelangelo and the Human Form: His Knowledge and Use of Anatomy", in *The Art Bulletin*, 7, 1984, pp. 176-86.

F. MANCINELLI and R. BELLINI, *Michelangiolo*, Florence 1992.

M. HIRST and J. DUNKERTON, *Making and Meaning: The Young Michelangelo*, New Haven-London 1994.

F. FALLETTI (ed.), *L'Accademia, Michelangelo, l'Ottocento*, Livorno 1997.

C. SEYMOUR, *Michelangelo's David. A Search for Identity*, Pittsburgh 1997.

G. BARTZ and E. KONIG, *Michelangelo*, Cologne 1998.

B. NARDINI, *Michelangelo. Biografia di un genio*, Florence 1999. English translation by C. Frost, *Michelangelo: Biography of a Genius*, Florence 1999.

K. WEIL-GARRIS BRANDT, C. ACIDINI LUCHINAT, J.D. DRAPER and N. PENNY (eds.), *Giovinezza di Michelangelo*, Florence-Milan 1999.

S. BRACCI, F. FALLETTI, M. MATTEINI and R. SCOPIGNO (eds.), *Exploring David. Diagnostic Tests and State of Conservation*, Florence 2004.

F. FALLETTI, *Il David di Michelangelo. Un capolavoro dopo il restauro*, Florence 2004. English translation by J. Reifsnyder, *Michelangelo's David: a Masterpiece Restored*, Florence 2004.

A. PAOLUCCI, G.M. RADKE and F. FALLETTI, "Michelangelo. Il David," in *Art Dossier*, July-August 2004.

G. DONATI, *Michelangelo*, Florence 2005.